Maths — No Problem!

Singapore Maths
English National Curriculum 2014

Consultant and Author
Dr. Yeap Ban Har

UK Consultant
Dr. Anne Hermanson

Authors
Dr. Foong Pui Yee
Lim Li Gek Pearlyn

Published by Maths — No Problem!
Copyright © 2017 by Maths — No Problem!

Printed in the United Kingdom
First Printing, 2014
Reprinted in 2015, twice in 2016 and once in 2017

ISBN 978-1-910504-04-8

Maths — No Problem!
Dowding House, Coach & Horses Passage
Tunbridge Wells, UK TN2 5NP
www.mathsnoproblem.co.uk

Acknowledgements

This Maths — No Problem! series, adapted from the New Syllabus
Primary Mathematics series, is published in collaboration with
Shing Lee Publishers. Pte Ltd.

Design and Illustration by Kin

Preface

Maths — No Problem! is a comprehensive series that adopts a spiral design with carefully built-up mathematical concepts and processes adapted from the maths mastery approaches used in Singapore. The Concrete-Pictorial-Abstract (C-P-A) approach forms an integral part of the learning process through the materials developed for this series.

Maths — No Problem! incorporates the use of concrete aids and manipulatives, problem-solving and group work.

In Maths — No Problem! Primary 3, these features are exemplified throughout the chapters:

Chapter Opener

Familiar events or occurrences that serve as an introduction for pupils.

In Focus

Includes questions related to various lesson objectives as an introductory activity for pupils.

There are 3 ways to colour the  .

Let's Learn

Introduces new concepts through a C-P-A approach with the use of engaging pictures and manipulatives. Guided examples are provided for reinforcement.

Activity Time

Provides pupils with opportunities to work as individuals or in small groups to explore mathematical concepts or to play games.

Guided Practice

Comprises questions for further consolidation and for the immediate evaluation of pupils' learning.

Mind Workout

Challenging non-routine questions for pupils to apply relevant heuristics and to develop higher-order thinking skills.

Maths Journal

Provides pupils with opportunities to show their understanding of the mathematical concepts learnt.

Self Check

Allows pupils to assess their own learning after each chapter.

I know how to...

☐ read the scales for mass in kg and g.
☐ solve word problems on mass.

Self Check

Contents

Chapter 3   **Multiplication and Division**

How many jelly beans are there altogether?

Chapter 1
Numbers to 1000

Counting in Hundreds

Recap

10 ones make 1 ten.

Use ▢ to show that 10 ones make 1 ten.
How many tens make 1 hundred?

In Focus

Count in hundreds.

How many jelly beans are there?

Let's Learn

Show the number of jelly beans using ▢▯.

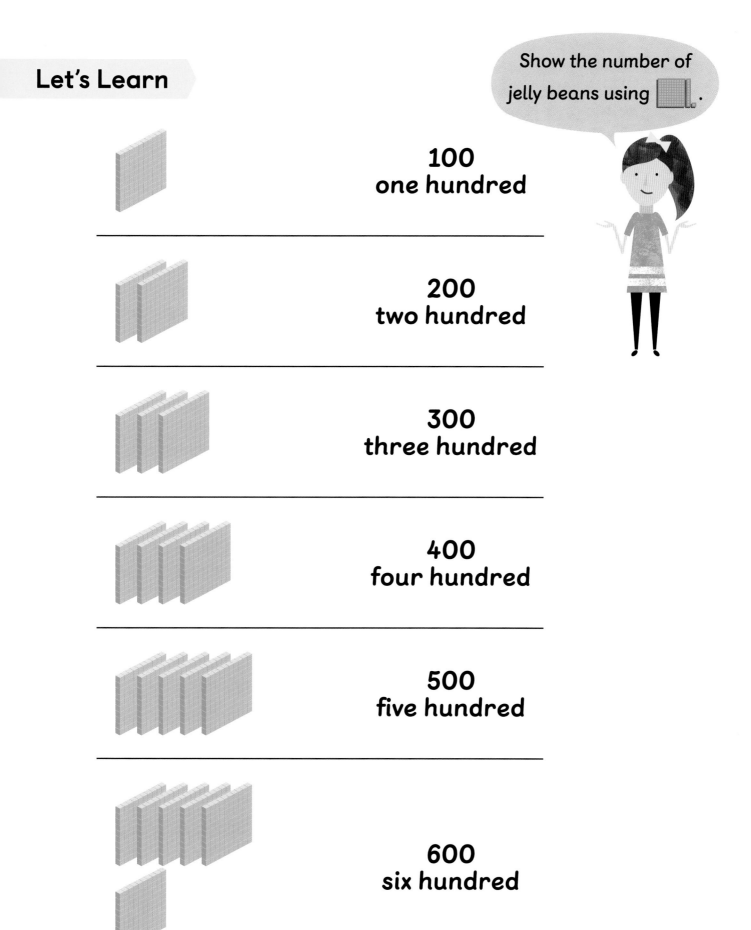

100
one hundred

200
two hundred

300
three hundred

400
four hundred

500
five hundred

600
six hundred

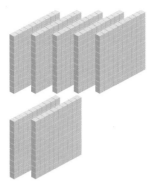

700
seven hundred

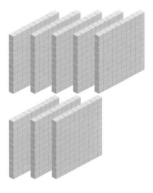

800
eight hundred

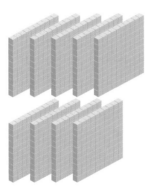

900
nine hundred

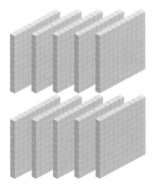

1000
one thousand

How many hundreds
make 1 thousand?

Guided Practice

Count.
Write in numbers and in words.

(a)

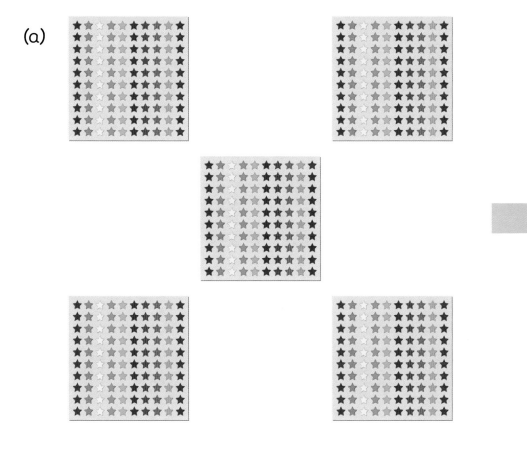

(b)

Complete Worksheet **1** – Page **1 - 2**

Counting in Hundreds, Tens and Ones

In Focus

How many beans are there altogether?

Let's Learn

1 How many are there?

100, 200, 201, 202, 203, 204

204
200   4

2 How many are there?

100, 200, 210, 220, 230

230
200   30

3 How many 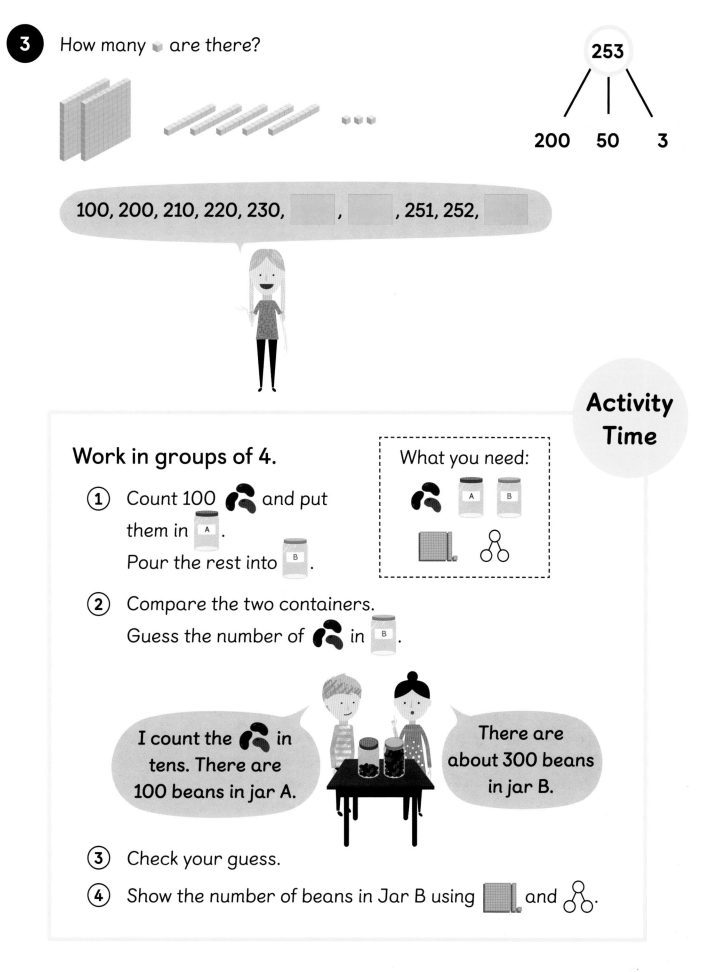 are there?

253
/ | \
200 50 3

100, 200, 210, 220, 230, [ ] , [ ] , 251, 252,

Activity Time

Work in groups of 4.

What you need:

① Count 100 🫘 and put them in [A].
Pour the rest into [B].

② Compare the two containers.
Guess the number of 🫘 in [B].

I count the 🫘 in tens. There are 100 beans in jar A.

There are about 300 beans in jar B.

③ Check your guess.

④ Show the number of beans in Jar B using ▦ and ⚬⚬.

Guided Practice

Count.
Write in numbers and fill in the number bonds.

(a)

(b)

Complete Worksheet **2** – Page **3 – 4**

Place Value

In Focus

There are 427 crayons.
What does the digit 4 in 427 stand for?

Let's Learn

1

The digit 4 is in the hundreds place. Which digit is in the tens place and in the ones place?

hundreds	tens	ones
4	2	7

427 = 4 hundreds + 2 tens + 7 ones
427 = 400 + 20 + 7

The digit 4 stands for 4 **hundreds** or 400.
The digit 2 stands for 2 **tens** or 20.
The digit 7 stands for 7 **ones** or 7.

We write 427 as **four hundred and twenty-seven**.

427

400   20   7

400
20
7

→   4 2 7

2 What is the value of each digit in 530?

hundreds	tens	ones
5	3	0

530

/ | \

500   30   0

530 = ☐ hundreds + ☐ tens + ☐ ones

530 = ☐ + ☐ + ☐

530

/ | \

500   20   10

The value of the digit 5 is 500.   500
The value of the digit 3 is 30.   30   →   5 3 0
The value of the digit 0 is 0.   0

We write 530 as **five hundred and thirty.**

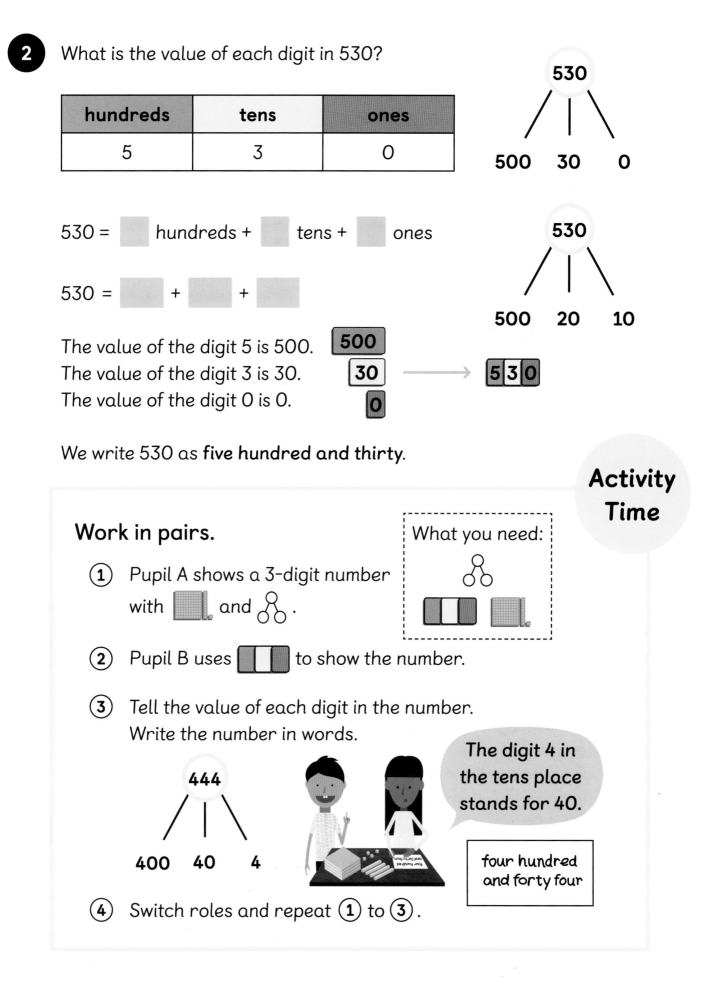

Activity Time

Work in pairs.

① Pupil A shows a 3-digit number with ▦ and 品.

What you need:

② Pupil B uses ▭ to show the number.

③ Tell the value of each digit in the number. Write the number in words.

444

/ | \

400   40   4

The digit 4 in the tens place stands for 40.

four hundred and forty four

④ Switch roles and repeat ① to ③.

Guided Practice

1 Count in hundreds, tens and ones.

hundreds	tens	ones

[ ] = [ ] hundreds + [ ] tens + [ ] ones

[ ] = [ ] + [ ] + [ ]

The digit [ ] is in the ones place.

The digit 3 stands for [ ] .

The value of the digit 5 is [ ] .

Show each number using /|\ .

2 Write in numerals.

(a)   five hundred and sixty-two

(b)   six hundred and forty

(c)   nine hundred and three

Do it in more than one way.

3 Write in words.

(a)   213   (b)   305

(c)   751   (d)   840

Complete Worksheet **3** – Page **5 - 8**

Comparing and Ordering Numbers

In Focus

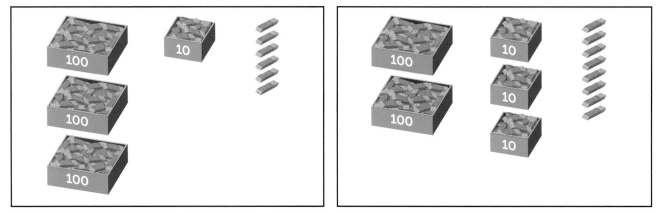

Shop A   Shop B

Which shop has more rubbers? How do you know?

Let's Learn

 1 Which number is greater, 316 or 238?

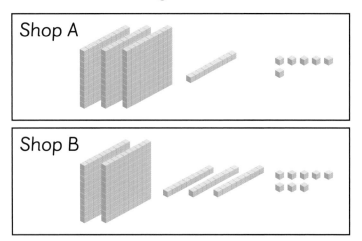

Shop A

Shop B

hundreds	tens	ones
3	1	6

hundreds	tens	ones
2	3	8

3 hundreds is more than 2 hundreds.
316 is more than 238.
Shop A has more rubbers.

What should we compare first?

2 Which number is smaller, 835 or 826?

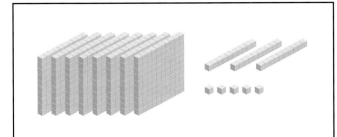

hundreds	tens	ones
8	3	5

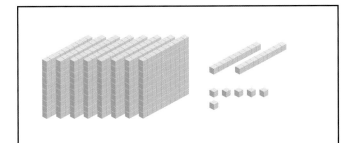

hundreds	tens	ones
8	2	6

The digits in the hundreds place are the same. What should we compare next?

We compare the digits in the tens place.

2 tens is less than 3 tens.
826 is less than 835.

Do you know how to compare 472 and 479? Which is greater?

3 Arrange 325, 235 and 253 in order.
Start with the smallest.

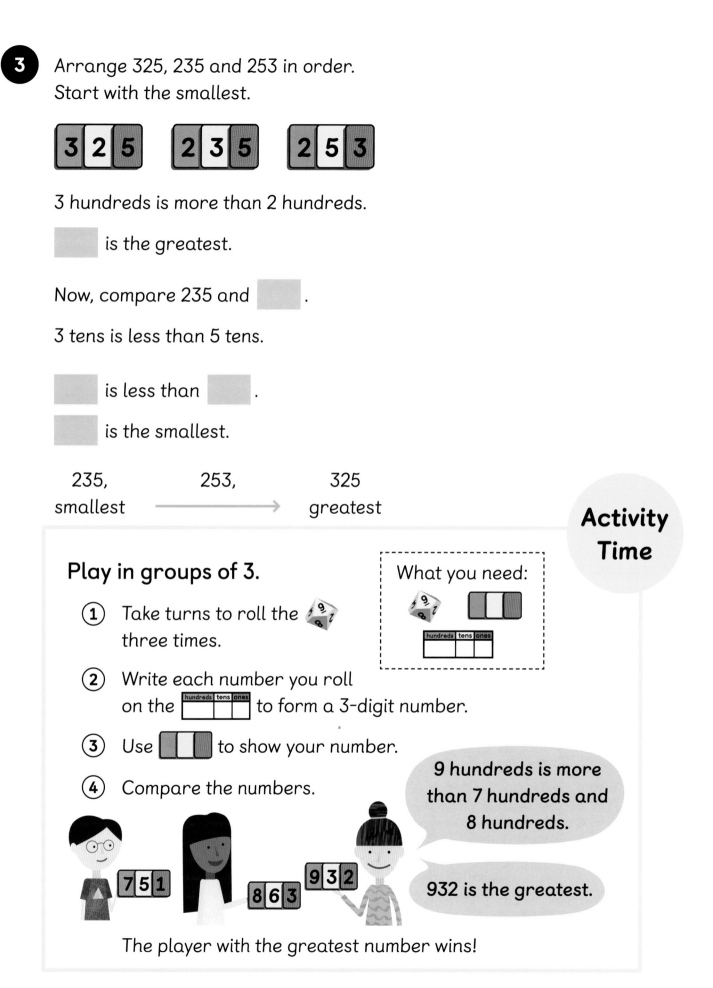

3 2 5   2 3 5   2 5 3

3 hundreds is more than 2 hundreds.

[   ] is the greatest.

Now, compare 235 and [   ].

3 tens is less than 5 tens.

[   ] is less than [   ].

[   ] is the smallest.

235,   253,   325
smallest ⟶   greatest

Activity Time

Play in groups of 3.

① Take turns to roll the 🎲 three times.

② Write each number you roll on the | hundreds | tens | ones | to form a 3-digit number.

③ Use ▦ to show your number.

④ Compare the numbers.

What you need:

🎲 ▦

| hundreds | tens | ones |

7 5 1   8 6 3   9 3 2

9 hundreds is more than 7 hundreds and 8 hundreds.

932 is the greatest.

The player with the greatest number wins!

Guided Practice

1 Compare the numbers.

(a)

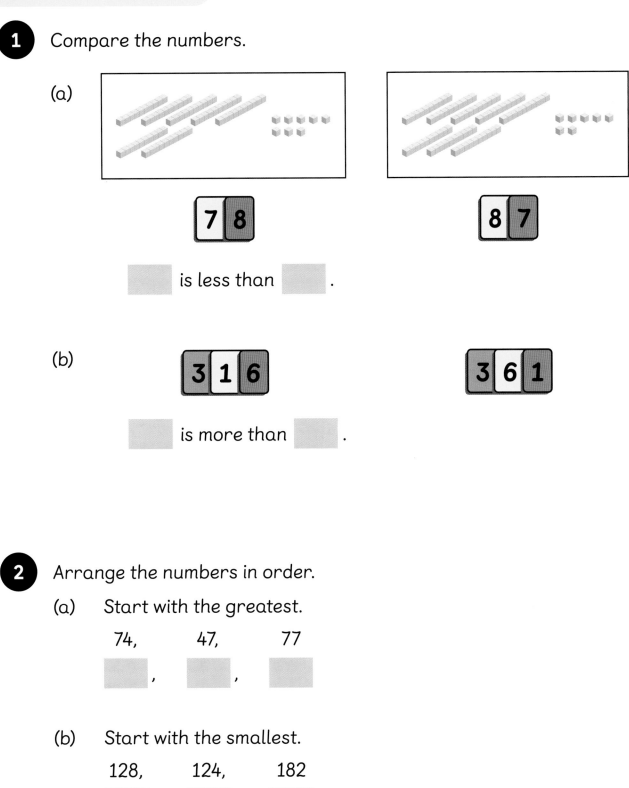

[7][8]   [8][7]

[____] is less than [____].

(b)   [3][1][6]   [3][6][1]

[____] is more than [____].

2 Arrange the numbers in order.

(a)   Start with the greatest.

74,   47,   77

[____] , [____] , [____]

(b)   Start with the smallest.

128,   124,   182

[____] , [____] , [____]

Complete Worksheet **4** – Page **9 – 13**

Counting in Fifties

In Focus

Each bundle has 50 straws.
How many straws are there?

Let's Learn

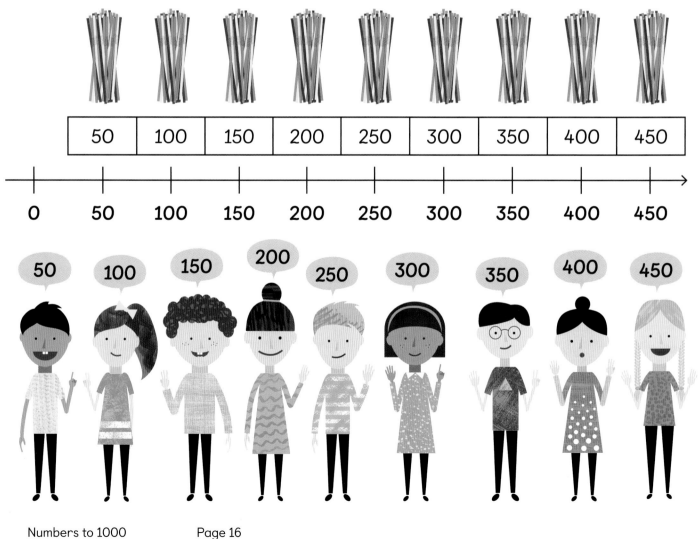

Play in groups of 4.

① Roll a dice.

② Count in fifties.
The number on the dice shows the number of fifties you need to count.

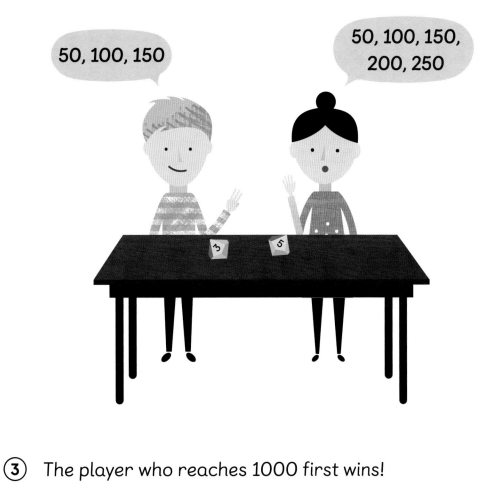

50, 100, 150

50, 100, 150,
200, 250

③ The player who reaches 1000 first wins!

Guided Practice

1 Count.
Write in numbers.

(a)

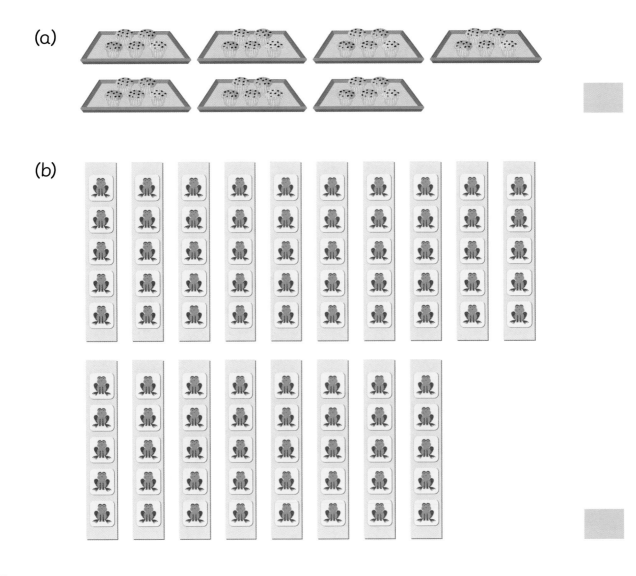

(b)

2 Complete the number patterns.

(a)

50	100	150	200	250		350	400	450

(b)

150	200			350		450		550

Complete Worksheet **5** – Page **14**

Number Patterns

Recap

Look at the number patterns.

11	12	13	14	?	16	17

100	99	98	97	?	95	94

What is the next number in each pattern?

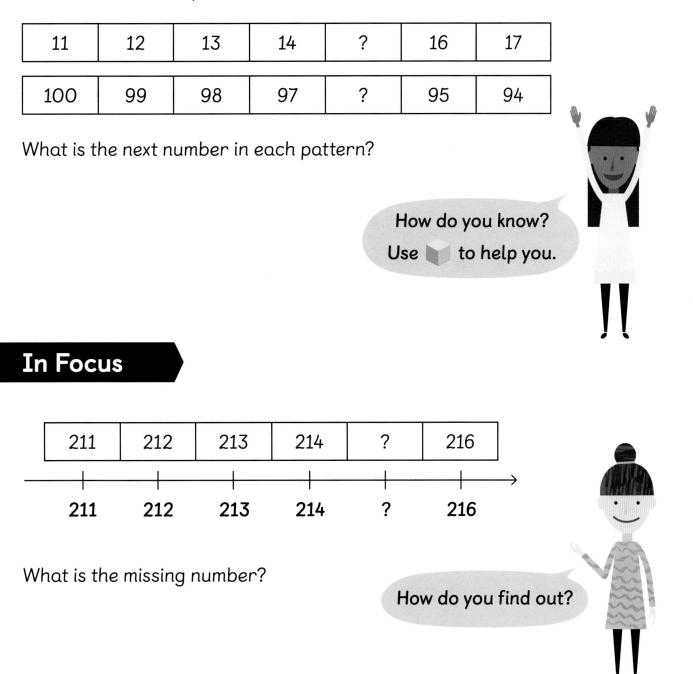

How do you know?
Use ⬛ to help you.

In Focus

211	212	213	214	?	216

211   212   213   214   ?   216

What is the missing number?

How do you find out?

Let's Learn

1

211	212	213	214	?	216

1 more 1 more 1 more

Use 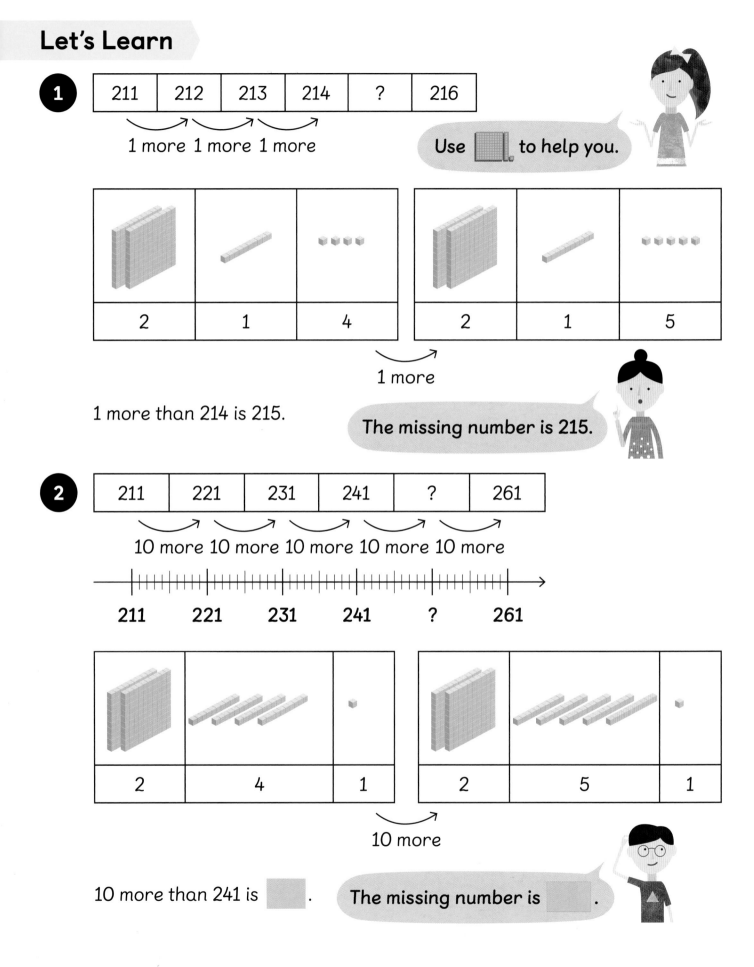 to help you.

2	1	4	2	1	5

1 more

1 more than 214 is 215.

The missing number is 215.

2

211	221	231	241	?	261

10 more 10 more 10 more 10 more 10 more

211   221   231   241   ?   261

2	4	1	2	5	1

10 more

10 more than 241 is ☐ .

The missing number is ☐ .

Guided Practice

1 Fill in the missing numbers.

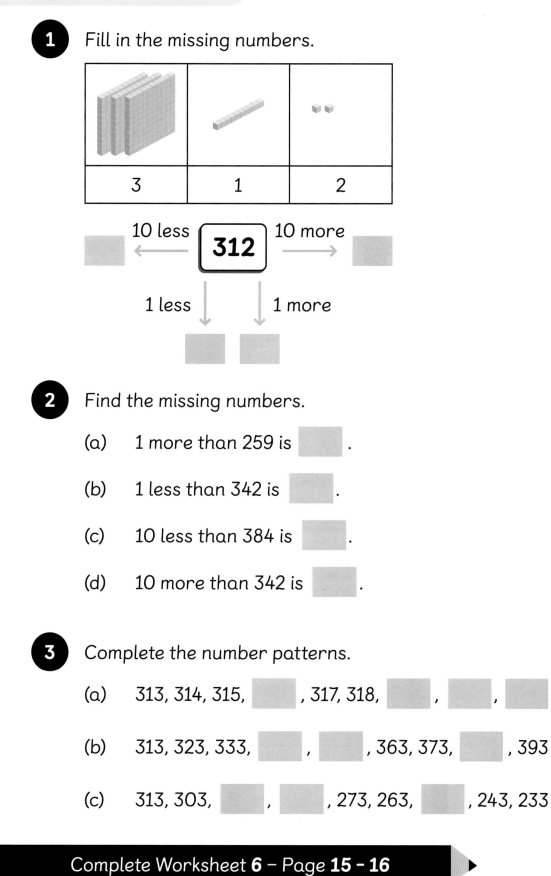

3	1	2

10 less ← **312** → 10 more

1 less ↓ 1 more ↓

2 Find the missing numbers.

(a)   1 more than 259 is ☐ .

(b)   1 less than 342 is ☐ .

(c)   10 less than 384 is ☐ .

(d)   10 more than 342 is ☐ .

3 Complete the number patterns.

(a)   313, 314, 315, ☐ , 317, 318, ☐ , ☐ , ☐ , 322

(b)   313, 323, 333, ☐ , ☐ , 363, 373, ☐ , 393

(c)   313, 303, ☐ , ☐ , 273, 263, ☐ , 243, 233

Complete Worksheet **6** – Page **15 – 16**

Number Patterns

In Focus

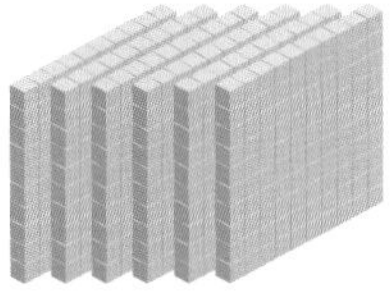 6	 4	5

What is 100 more than 645?
What is 100 less than 645?

Let's Learn

1

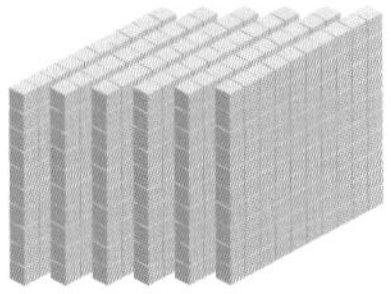 6	 4	 5

↓ 100 more

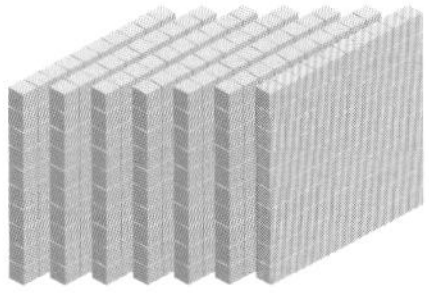 7	 4	5

100 more than 645 is 745.

2

7	4	5

↓ 100 more

8	4	5

100 more than 745 is 845.

3

8	4	5

↓ 100 more

9	4	5

100 more than 845 is 945.
What do you notice?

100 less than 645 is ___ .

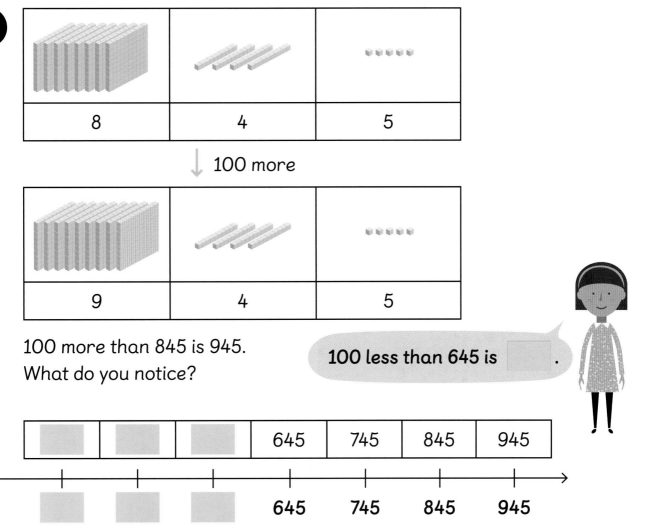

			645	745	845	945

645   745   845   945

Guided Practice

1 Fill in the missing numbers.

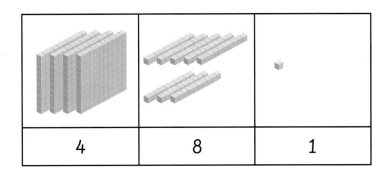

4	8	1

100 less ←————— **481** —————→ 100 more

2 Find the missing numbers.

(a) 100 more than 479 is ▢ .

(b) 100 less than 479 is ▢ .

(c) 100 more than 179 is ▢ .

(d) 100 less than 179 is ▢ .

3 Complete the number patterns.

(a) 768, 668, 568, ▢ , ▢ , 268

(b) 112, ▢ , ▢ , 412, 512, 612

(c) ▢ , ▢ , 645, 745, 845, 945

Complete Worksheet 7 – Page 17 – 18 ▶

Counting in Fours and Eights

In Focus

How many coins are there?

Let's Learn

1

100

Count in ones.
101, 102, 103, 104, 105, 106,
107, 108, 109, 110, 111, 112,
113, 114, 115, 116, 117, 118,
119, 120, 121, 122, 123, 124.

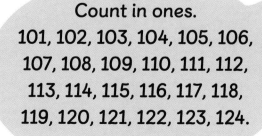

There are 124 coins.

2

100

Count in fours.
104, 108, 112, 116, 120, 124.

There are 124 coins.

3

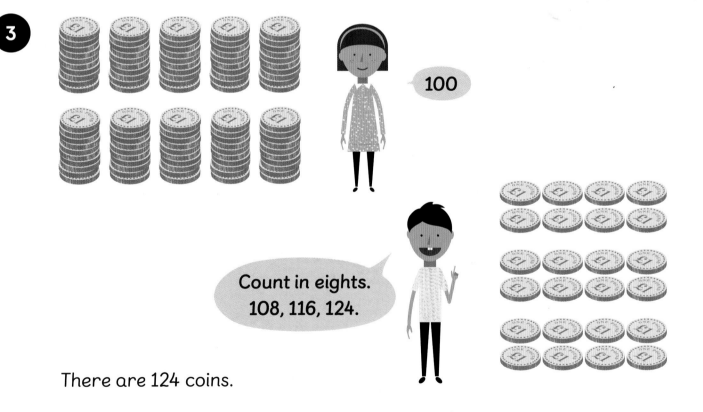

100

Count in eights.
108, 116, 124.

There are 124 coins.

Guided Practice

1 Count in fours.

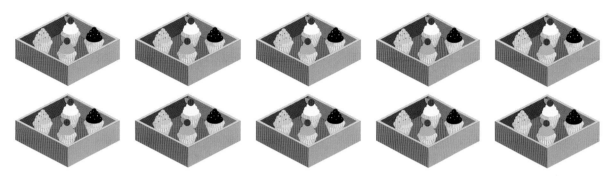

2 Count in eights.

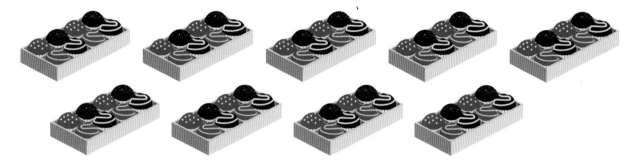

Complete Worksheet 8 – Page 19 - 21 ▶

Mind Workout ▶

Charles is thinking of a 3-digit number.
The digit in the ones place is the smallest odd digit.
The digit in the tens place is the greatest even digit.

**What is the smallest odd digit?
What is the greatest even digit?**

What is the number?

Maths Journal

Look for 3-digit numbers around you.

What are some of the ways that numbers are used around you?

Why do we use numbers?

I know how to...

☐ count to 1000.

☐ count in hundreds, tens and ones.

☐ count in fifties.

☐ count in fours and eights.

☐ tell the value of a digit in a number.

☐ compare and arrange numbers within 1000.

☐ complete number patterns.

How many chairs are there in the classroom altogether?

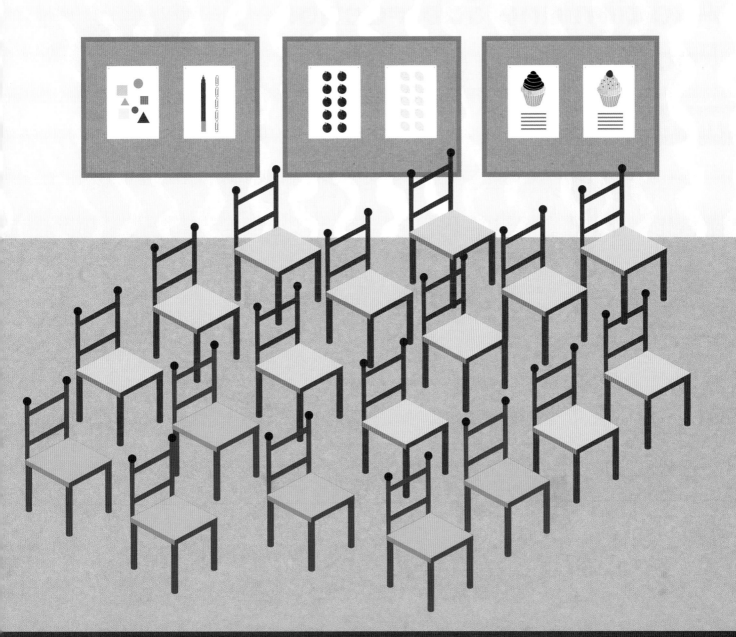

Chapter 2
Addition and Subtraction

Addition and Subtraction Facts

In Focus

6 blue chairs

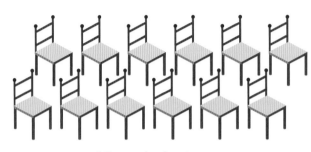

12 red chairs

How many chairs are there altogether?

When do we add or subtract?

Let's Learn

| 6 + 12 = 18 | or | 12 + 6 = 18 |

There are 18 chairs altogether.

| 18 − 12 = 6 |

There are 6 blue chairs.

| 18 − 6 = 12 |

There are 12 red chairs.

We add to find the total.
We subtract to find the parts.

We can write a family of addition and subtraction facts.

6 + 12 = 18   18 − 12 = 6

12 + 6 = 18   18 − 6 = 12

Work in pairs.

What you need:

① Deal two ⑨.

② Write an addition equation.
Get your partner to write a family of addition and subtraction facts.

③ Use the family of facts to tell number stories.

> I have 9 sweets. Charles has 5 sweets. We have 14 sweets altogether.

$9 + 5 = 14$ $14 - 5 = 9$

$5 + 9 = 14$ $14 - 9 = 5$

$9 + 5 = 14$

④ Take turns to repeat ① to ③.

Activity Time

Complete Worksheet 1 · Page 27 – 28

Simple Adding

In Focus

There were 213 books in the bookcase.
How many books were there after Hannah put 4 more books in it?

Let's Learn

Add 213 and 4.

Method 1   Count on from 213.

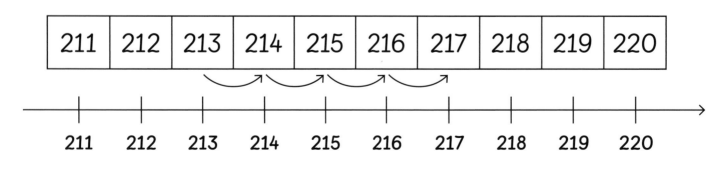

213 + 4 = 217

Method 2   Add the ones.

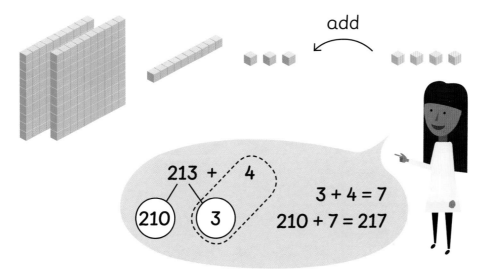

$3 + 4 = 7$

$210 + 7 = 217$

$213 + 4 = 217$

There were 217 books in the bookcase.

Guided Practice

1 Add 121 and 4.

$121 + 4 = $ ▢

2 Add 3 and 492.

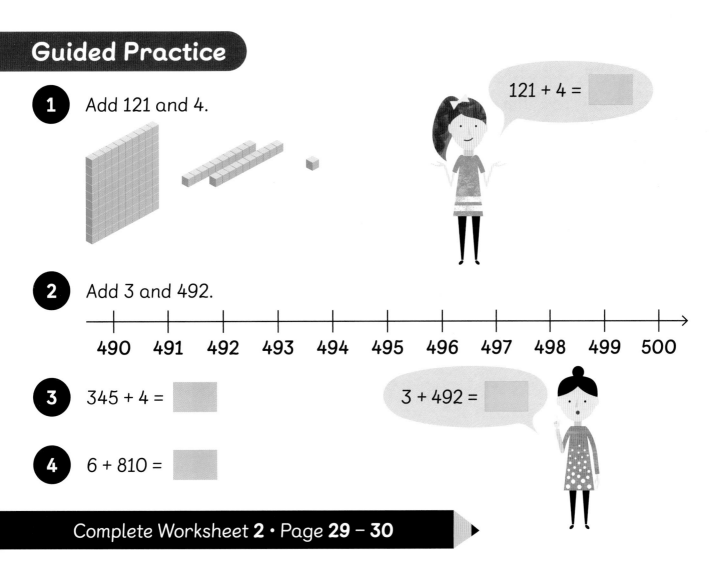

490   491   492   493   494   495   496   497   498   499   500

3 $345 + 4 = $ ▢

$3 + 492 = $ ▢

4 $6 + 810 = $ ▢

Complete Worksheet 2 · Page 29 – 30

Simple Adding

In Focus

In a school hall, there are 119 girls and 80 boys.
How many pupils are there altogether?

Let's Learn

 Add 119 and 80.

Method 1   Count on in tens from 119.

119 + 80 = 199

119, 129, 139, 149, 159, 169, 179, 189, 199

Is there another way to add the numbers?

Method 2   Add the tens.

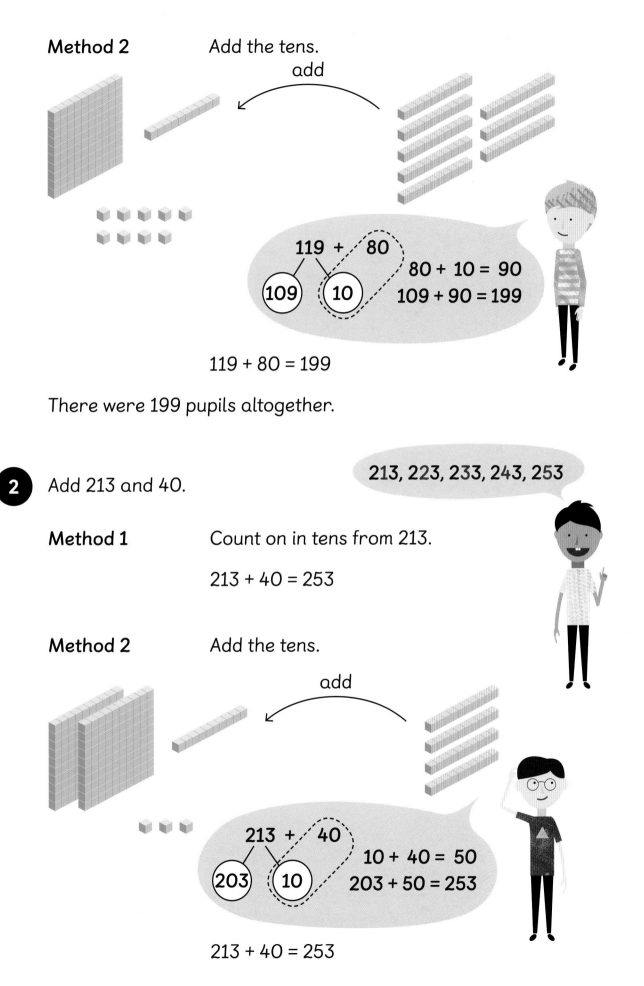

add

119 + 80

(109)   (10)

80 + 10 = 90
109 + 90 = 199

119 + 80 = 199

There were 199 pupils altogether.

2 Add 213 and 40.

213, 223, 233, 243, 253

Method 1   Count on in tens from 213.

213 + 40 = 253

Method 2   Add the tens.

add

213 + 40

(203)   (10)

10 + 40 = 50
203 + 50 = 253

213 + 40 = 253

Guided Practice

1 Add 734 and 20.

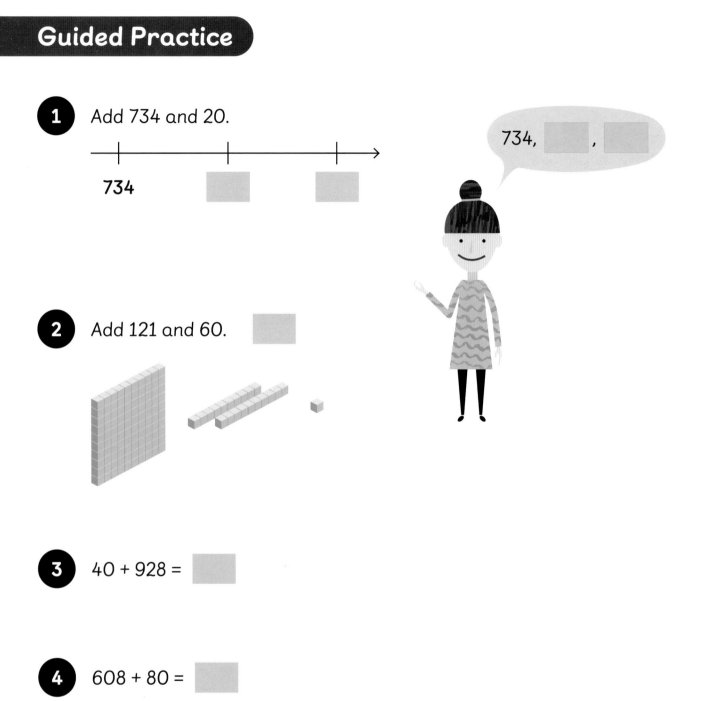

734, ⬜ , ⬜

2 Add 121 and 60.

3 40 + 928 = ⬜

4 608 + 80 = ⬜

Complete Worksheet **3** · Page **31 – 32**

Simple Adding

In Focus

Evergreen Primary School has 213 pupils.
There are 400 more pupils in Lakeside Primary School than in Evergreen Primary School.

How many pupils are there in Lakeside Primary School?

Let's Learn

213, 313, 413, 513, 613

Add 213 and 400.

Method 1   Count on in hundreds from 213.

213 + 400 = 613

Method 2

Add the hundreds.

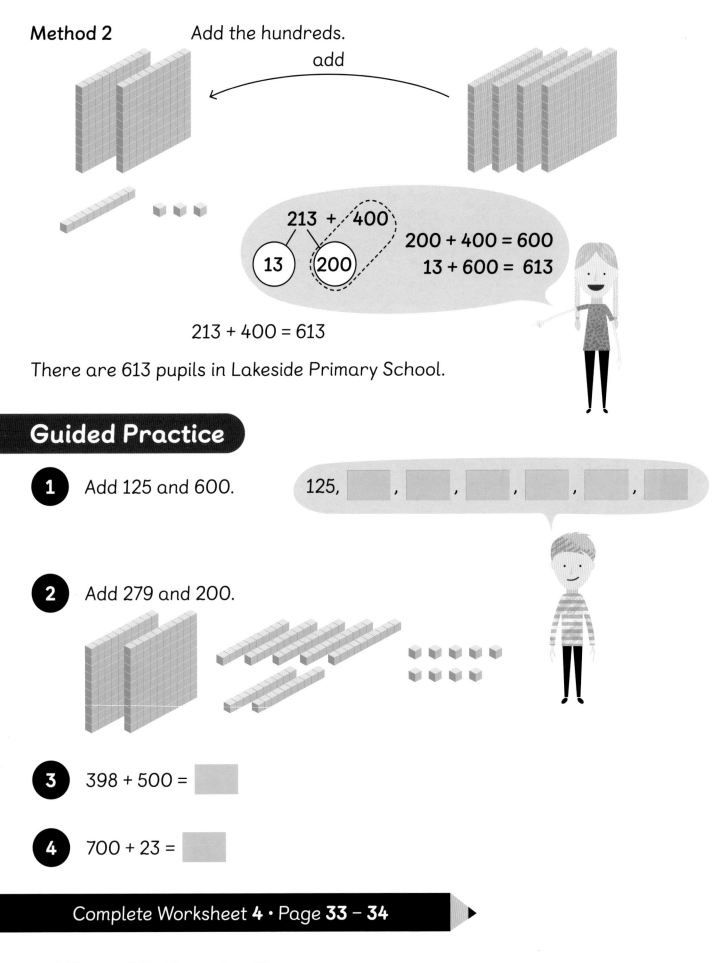

add

213 + 400

13 200

200 + 400 = 600

13 + 600 = 613

213 + 400 = 613

There are 613 pupils in Lakeside Primary School.

Guided Practice

1 Add 125 and 600.

125, ☐ , ☐ , ☐ , ☐ , ☐ , ☐

2 Add 279 and 200.

3 398 + 500 = ☐

4 700 + 23 = ☐

Complete Worksheet 4 · Page 33 – 34

Simple Adding

In Focus

432 flowers

521 flowers

How many flowers are there altogether?

Let's Learn

Add 432 and 521.

Use  to help you add.

Step 1   Add the ones.
2 ones + 1 one = 3 ones

h	t	o
4	3	2
+ 5	2	1
		3

Step 2   Add the tens.
           3 tens + 2 tens = 5 tens

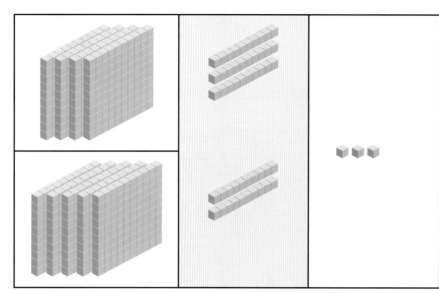

	h	t	o
	4	3	2
+	5	2	1
		5	3

Step 3   Add the hundreds.
           4 hundreds + 5 hundreds = 9 hundreds

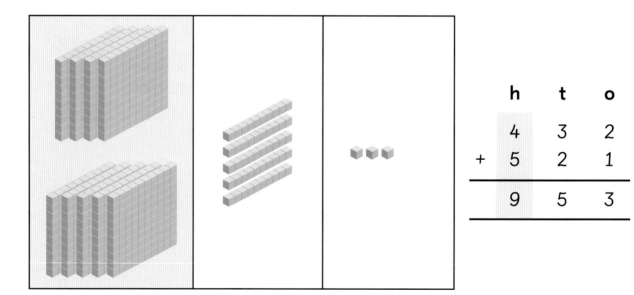

	h	t	o
	4	3	2
+	5	2	1
	9	5	3

432 + 521 = 953

There are 953 flowers altogether.

Add.

1 (a) 153 + 2 = ▢

(b) 153 + 20 = ▢

(c) 153 + 200 = ▢

2 (a) 214 + 3 = ▢

(b) 214 + 30 = ▢

(c) 214 + 300 = ▢

3 (a) 325 + 14 = ▢

h	t	o
3	2	5
+	1	4
▢	▢	▢

(b) 236 + 543 = ▢

h	t	o
2	3	6
+ 5	4	3
▢	▢	▢

(c) 457 + 432 = ▢

h	t	o
4	5	7
+ 4	3	2
▢	▢	▢

(d) 500 + 171 = ▢

h	t	o
5	0	0
+ 1	7	1
▢	▢	▢

(e) 31 + 448 = ▢

h	t	o
▢	▢	▢
+ ▢	▢	▢
▢	▢	▢

(f) 605 + 384 = ▢

h	t	o
▢	▢	▢
+ ▢	▢	▢
▢	▢	▢

Complete Worksheet 5 · Page 35 – 36

Adding with Renaming

In Focus

8 children joined a group of 236 children.

How many children are there altogether?

Let's Learn

Add 8 and 236.

Method 1

Step 1	Add the ones.		h	t	o
					8
	8 + 6 = 14	+	2	3	6
				1	4

Step 2	Add the tens.		h	t	o
					8
	0 + 30 = 30	+	2	3	6
				1	4
		+		3	0

Step 3	Add the hundreds.		h	t	o
					8
	0 + 200 = 200	+	2	3	6
				1	4
				3	0

Step 4	Add 14, 30 and 200	+	2	0	0
	8 + 236 = 244		2	4	4

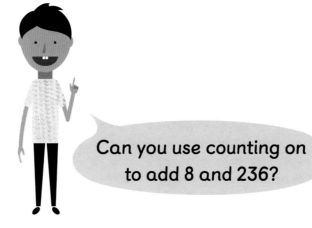

Can you use counting on to add 8 and 236?

Method 2

Step 1   Add the ones.

8 ones + 6 ones = 14 ones

8 + 6 = 14

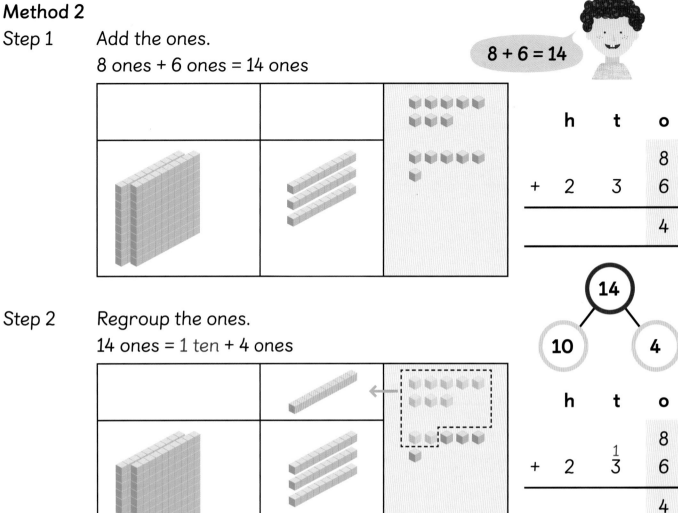

	h	t	o
			8
+	2	3	6
			4

Step 2   Regroup the ones.

14 ones = 1 ten + 4 ones

	h	t	o
			8
+	2	$\overset{1}{3}$	6
			4

Step 3   Add the tens.

1 ten + 3 tens = 4 tens

Add the hundreds.

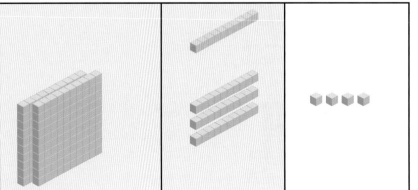

	h	t	o
			8
+	2	$\overset{1}{3}$	6
	2	4	4

8 + 236 = 244

There are 244 children altogether.

Method 3

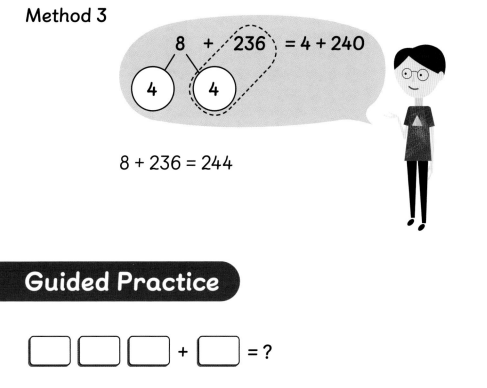

$8 + 236 = 244$

Guided Practice

Use 2 7 9 6 to make two numbers.
Add the numbers.

Example

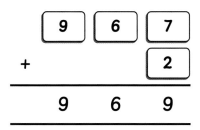

$967 + 2 = 969$

Complete Worksheet 6 · Page 37 – 38

Adding with Renaming

In Focus

| 2 | 7 | 9 | 6 |

| | | | + | | 0 |

Make two numbers using | 2 | 7 | 9 | 6 |.

Add them to get a total.

How many different totals less than 1000 can you get?

Let's Learn

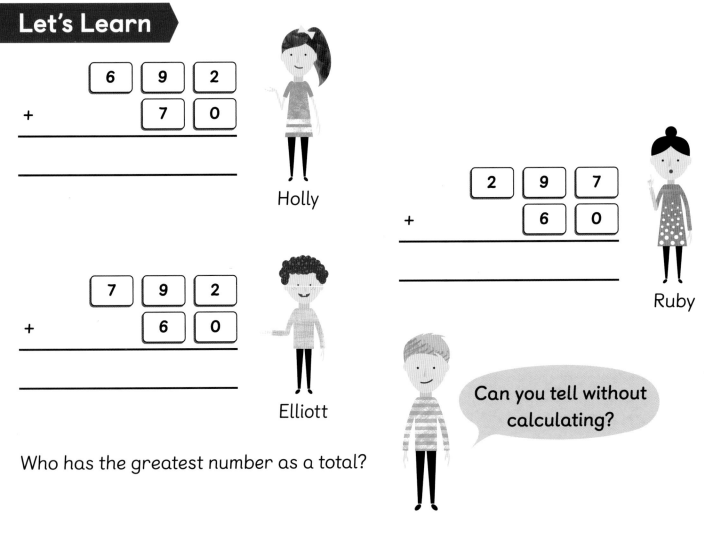

| 6 | 9 | 2 |
| + | 7 | 0 |

Holly

| 2 | 9 | 7 |
| + | 6 | 0 |

Ruby

| 7 | 9 | 2 |
| + | 6 | 0 |

Elliott

Can you tell without calculating?

Who has the greatest number as a total?

1 Add 692 and 70.

Use 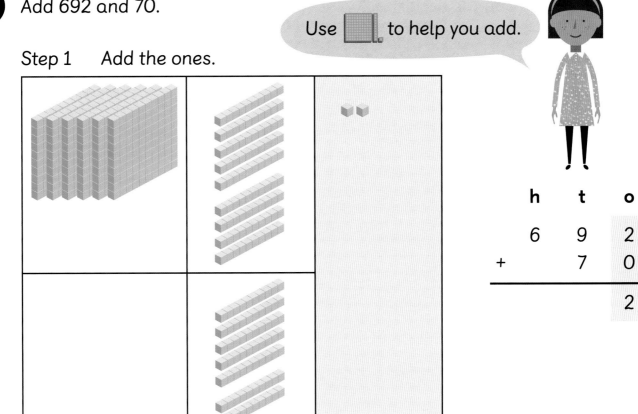 to help you add.

Step 1   Add the ones.

	h	t	o
	6	9	2
+		7	0
			2

Step 2   Add the tens.
9 tens + 7 tens = 16 tens
Regroup the tens.
16 tens = 1 hundred + 6 tens

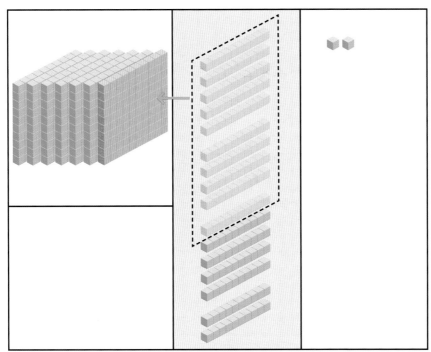

	h	t	o
	6	9	2
+		7	0
			2
	1	6	0

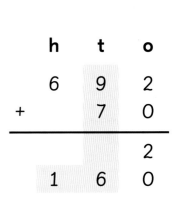

Step 3   Add the hundreds.

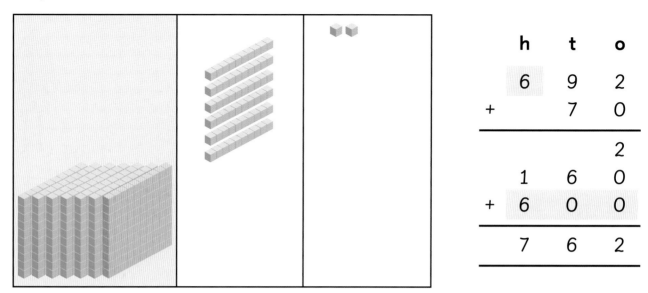

	h	t	o
	6	9	2
+		7	0
			2
	1	6	0
+	6	0	0
	7	6	2

Step 4   Add 2, 160 and 600

692 + 70 = 762

2   Add 792 and 60.

Step 1   Add the ones.

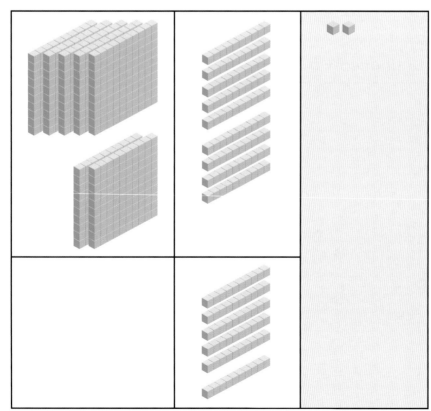

	h	t	o
	7	9	2
+		6	0
			2

Step 2   Add the tens.
9 tens + 6 tens = 15 tens
Regroup the tens.
15 tens = 1 hundred + 5 tens

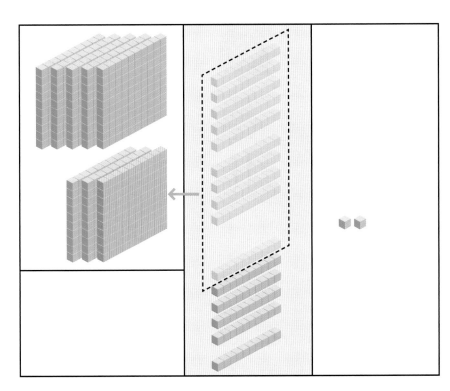

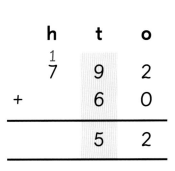

h	t	o
¹7	9	2
+	6	0
	5	2

Step 3   Add the hundreds.
1 hundred + 7 hundreds = 8 hundreds

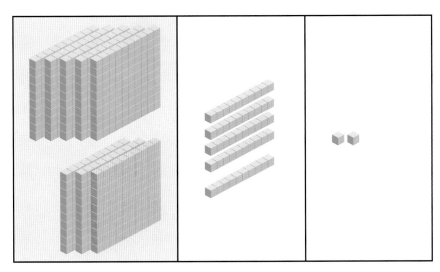

h	t	o
¹7	9	2
+	6	0
8	5	2

792 + 60 = 852

3 Add 297 and 60.

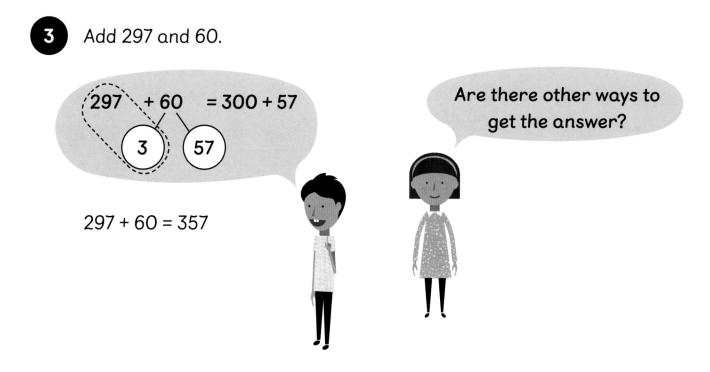

297 + 60 = 300 + 57

3   57

297 + 60 = 357

Are there other ways to get the answer?

4 692 + 70 is more than 700 but less than 800.

792 + 60 is more than 800 but less than 900.

297 + 60 is more than 300 but less than 400.

692 is about 700.

792 is about 800.

297 is about 300.

Holly

Elliott

Ruby

Elliott has the greatest number as a total.

1

| 8 | 5 | 4 | 6 |

| | | | + | | 0 |

Make 2 numbers using | 8 | 5 | 4 | 6 |.

Add them to get a total.

(a)   Show 5 more ways to do it.

(b)   What is the greatest total?

(c)   What is the smallest total?

2   Estimate the total.

(a)   397 + 90

(b)   10 + 599

397 is about   .

599 is about   .

Complete Worksheet **7** · Page **39 – 40**

Adding with Renaming

In Focus

6 ones + 5 ones = 11 ones

$$\begin{array}{r} 2\ 3\ 6 \\ +\ 3\ 4\ 5 \\ \hline \end{array}$$

What should Hannah do next?

Let's Learn

Add 236 and 345.

Use [ ] to help you add.

Step 1   Add the ones.
6 ones + 5 ones = 11 ones
Regroup the ones.
11 ones = 1 ten + 1 one

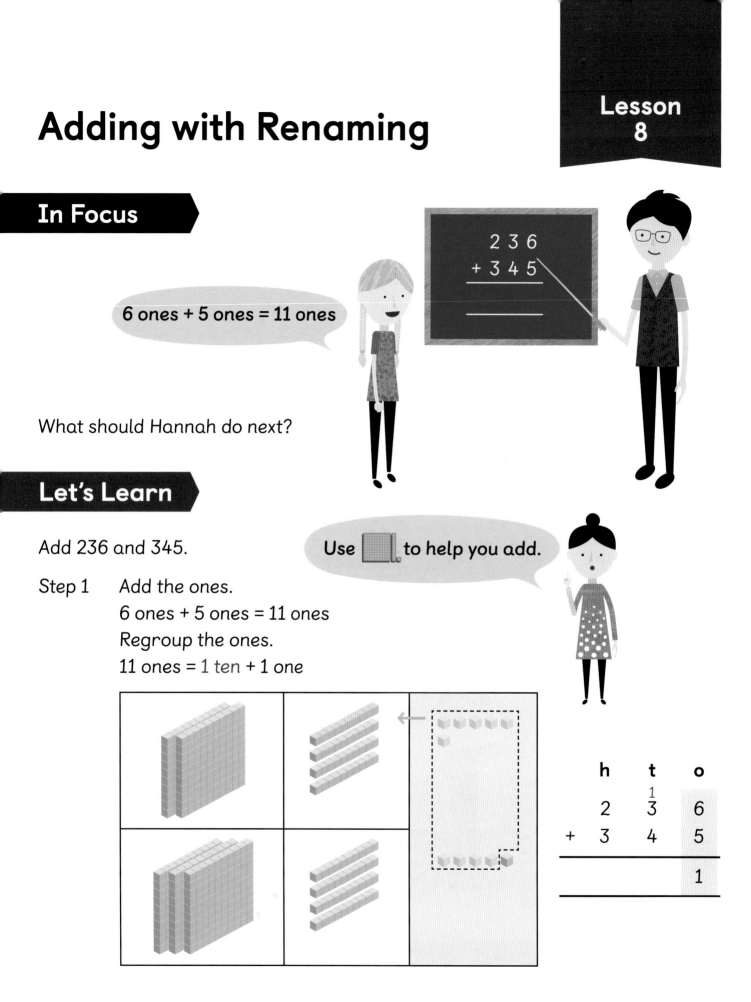

	h	t	o
		1	
	2	3	6
+	3	4	5
			1

Step 2   Add the tens.

1 ten + 3 tens + 4 tens = 8 tens

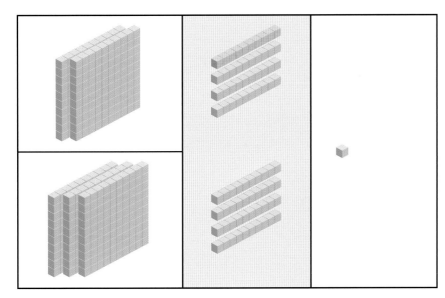

	h	t	o
		1	
	2	3	6
+	3	4	5
		8	1

Step 3   Add the hundreds.

2 hundreds + 3 hundreds = 5 hundreds

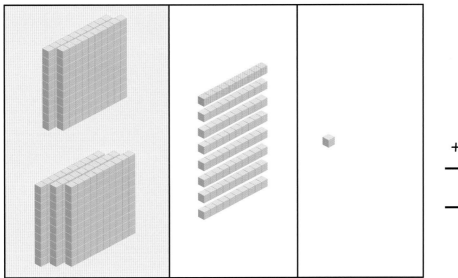

	h	t	o
		1	
	2	3	6
+	3	4	5
	5	8	1

236 + 345 = 581

1 Add.

(a)   423 and 135

$$
\begin{array}{cccc}
 & 4 & 2 & 3 \\
+ & 1 & 3 & 5 \\
\hline
 & \boxed{} & \boxed{} & \boxed{} \\
\hline
\end{array}
$$

(b)   423 and 138

$$
\begin{array}{cccc}
 & 4 & 2 & 3 \\
+ & 1 & 3 & 8 \\
\hline
 & \boxed{} & \boxed{} & \boxed{} \\
\hline
\end{array}
$$

2 Add.

(a)   234 + 155 = ☐

$$
\begin{array}{cccc}
 & 2 & 3 & 4 \\
+ & 1 & 5 & 5 \\
\hline
 & \boxed{} & \boxed{} & \boxed{} \\
\hline
\end{array}
$$

(b)   27 + 345 = ☐

$$
\begin{array}{cccc}
 & & 2 & 7 \\
+ & 3 & 4 & 5 \\
\hline
 & \boxed{} & \boxed{} & \boxed{} \\
\hline
\end{array}
$$

3 Add 23 and 147.

Complete Worksheet **8** · Page **41 – 42**

Adding with Renaming

In Focus

Lulu made 236 chocolate cookies and 391 vanilla cookies.

How can we find the total number of cookies Lulu made?

Let's Learn

Add 236 and 391.

Step 1   Add the ones.
6 ones + 1 one = 7 ones

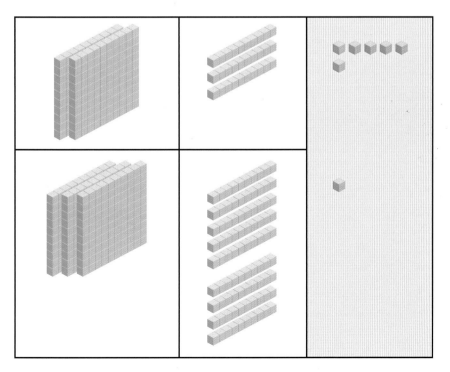

	h	t	o
	2	3	6
+	3	9	1
			7

Step 2 Add the tens.

3 tens + 9 tens = 12 tens

Regroup the tens.

12 tens = 1 hundred + 2 tens

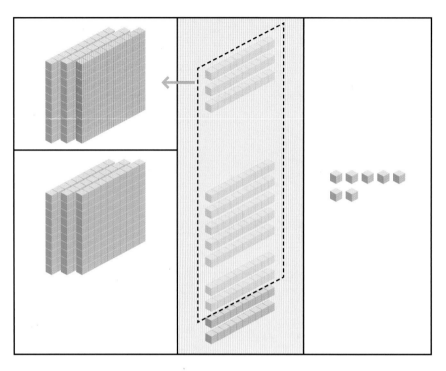

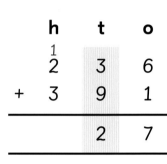

	h	t	o
	$\overset{1}{2}$	3	6
+	3	9	1
		2	7

Step 3 Add the hundreds.

1 hundred + 2 hundreds + 3 hundreds = 6 hundreds

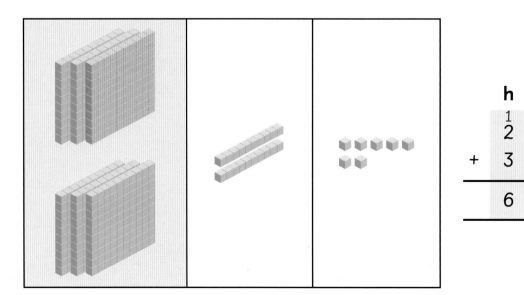

	h	t	o
	$\overset{1}{2}$	3	6
+	3	9	1
	6	2	7

236 + 391 = 627

Lulu made 627 cookies.

Guided Practice

1 Add.

(a) 132 and 157

```
      1   3   2
  +   1   5   7
  _____
     [  ][  ][  ]
  _____
```

(b) 132 and 187

```
      1   3   2
  +   1   8   7
  _____
     [  ][  ][  ]
  _____
```

2 Add.

(a) 301 + 197 = [ ]

```
      3   0   1
  +   1   9   7
  _____
     [  ][  ][  ]
  _____
```

(b) 24 + 591 = [ ]

```
          2   4
  +   5   9   1
  _____
     [  ][  ][  ]
  _____
```

3 Add 97 and 182.

Complete Worksheet **9** • Page **43 – 44**

Adding with Renaming

In Focus

Holly used | 2 | 3 | 4 | 7 | 8 | 9 | to make two numbers.

What is the sum of the two numbers?

| 2 | 7 | 8 | | 3 | 4 | 9 |

Let's Learn

Add 278 and 349.

The sum is the the total of 278 and 349.

Step 1   Add the ones.
8 ones + 9 ones = 17 ones
Regroup the ones.
17 ones = 1 ten + 7 ones

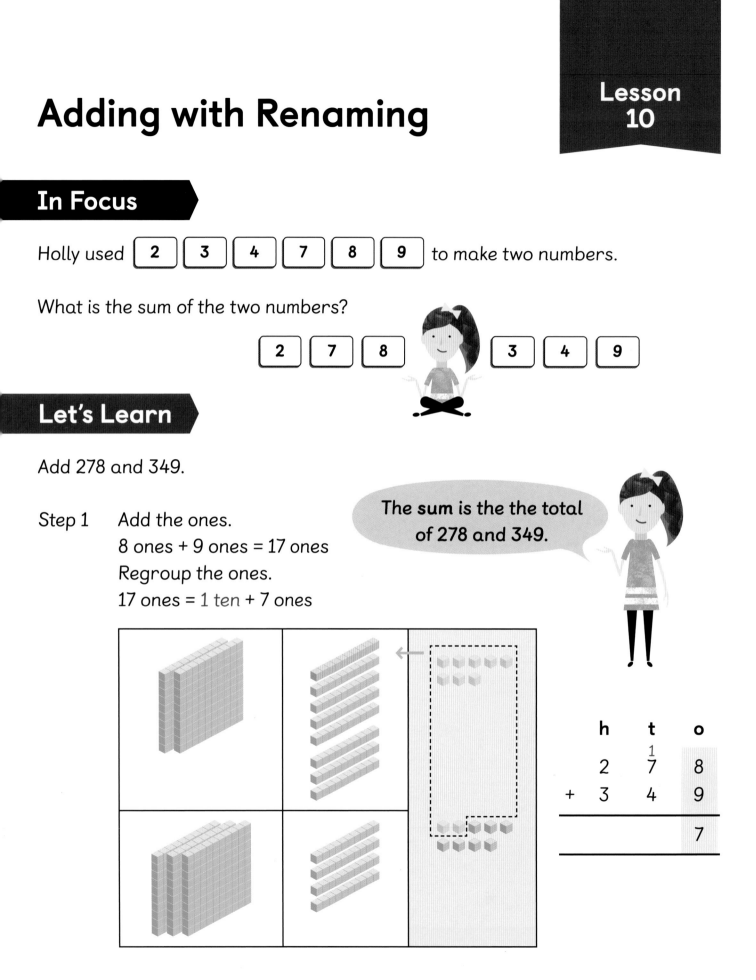

h	t	o
	$\overset{1}{7}$	
2	7	8
+ 3	4	9
		7

Step 2 Add the tens.

1 ten + 7 tens + 4 tens = 12 tens

Regroup the tens.

12 tens = 1 hundred + 2 tens

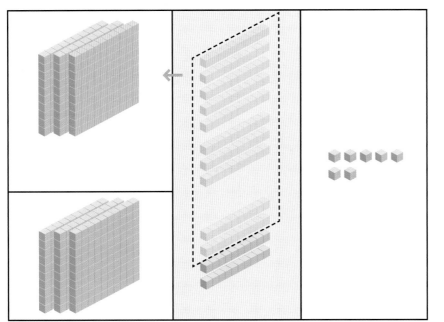

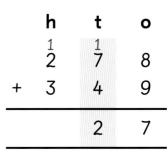

h	t	o
¹	¹	
2	7	8
+ 3	4	9
	2	7

Step 3 Add the hundreds.

1 hundred + 2 hundreds + 3 hundreds = 6 hundreds

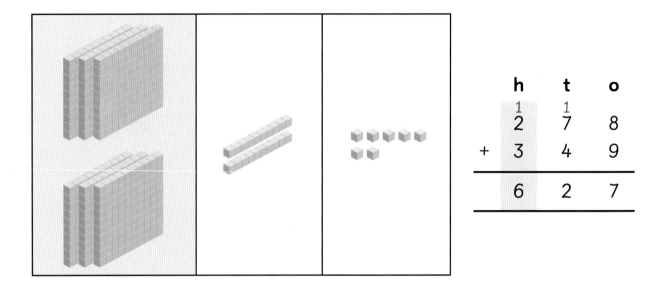

$$278 + 349 = 627$$

Work in pairs.

Use 2 3 4 7 8 9
to make other addition equations.

What you need:

2 3 4
7 8 9

The sum must be less than 1000.

Complete Worksheet **10** · Page **45 – 46**

Simple Subtracting

In Focus

Sam had 58 cookies.
He ate 4 cookies.
How many cookies did he have left?

Let's Learn

Subtract 4 from 58.

Method 1   Count back from 58.

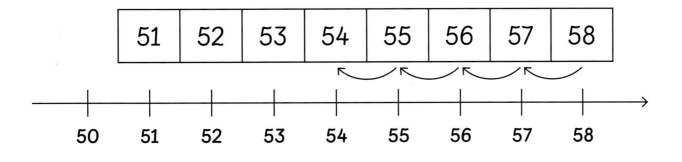

$$58 - 4 = 54$$

Method 2   Subtract ones.

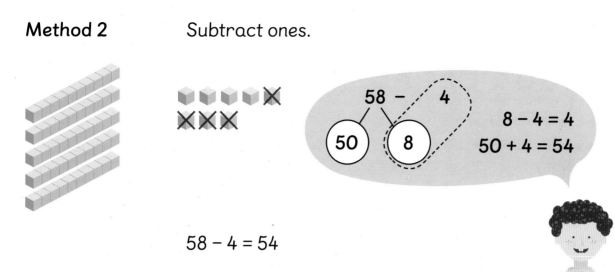

$$58 - 4 = 54$$

Sam had 54 cookies left.

Guided Practice

Subtract.

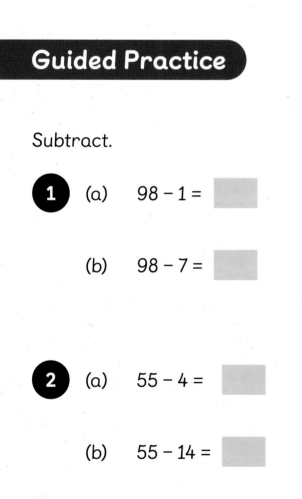

1 (a) $98 - 1 = $ ⬜

  (b) $98 - 7 = $ ⬜

2 (a) $55 - 4 = $ ⬜

  (b) $55 - 14 = $ ⬜

Complete Worksheet **11** • Page **47 – 48**

Simple Subtracting

In Focus

There were 658 chairs in the school hall.
Ruby took 4 chairs away.
How many chairs are there now?

Let's Learn

Subtract 4 from 658.

Method 1   Count back from 658.

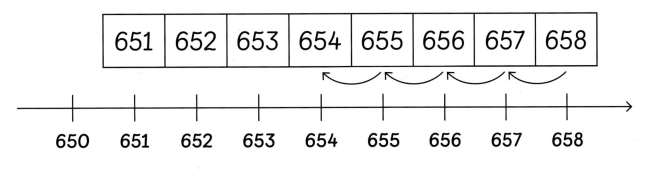

658 − 4 = 654

Method 2   Subtract ones.

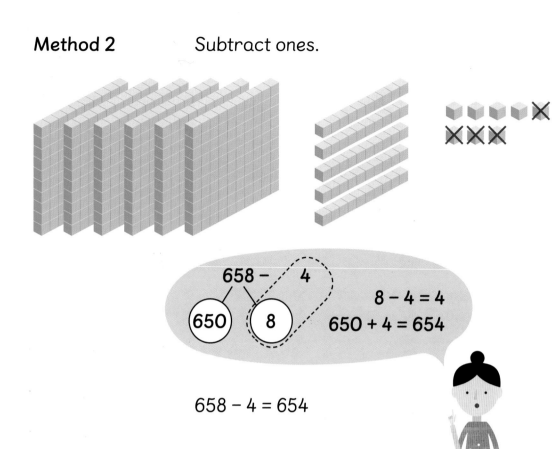

$$658 - 4 = 654$$

There are 654 chairs now.

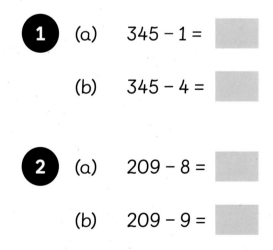

Guided Practice

Subtract.

1 (a) $345 - 1 =$ ☐

  (b) $345 - 4 =$ ☐

2 (a) $209 - 8 =$ ☐

  (b) $209 - 9 =$ ☐

Complete Worksheet **12** · Page **49 – 50**

Simple Subtracting

In Focus

There were 658 children at a concert.
40 left the hall during the interval.
How many children remained in the hall?

Let's Learn

Subtract 40 from 658.

Method 1   Count back in tens from 658.

658 − 40 = 618

658, 648, 638, 628, 618

Method 2   Subtract tens.

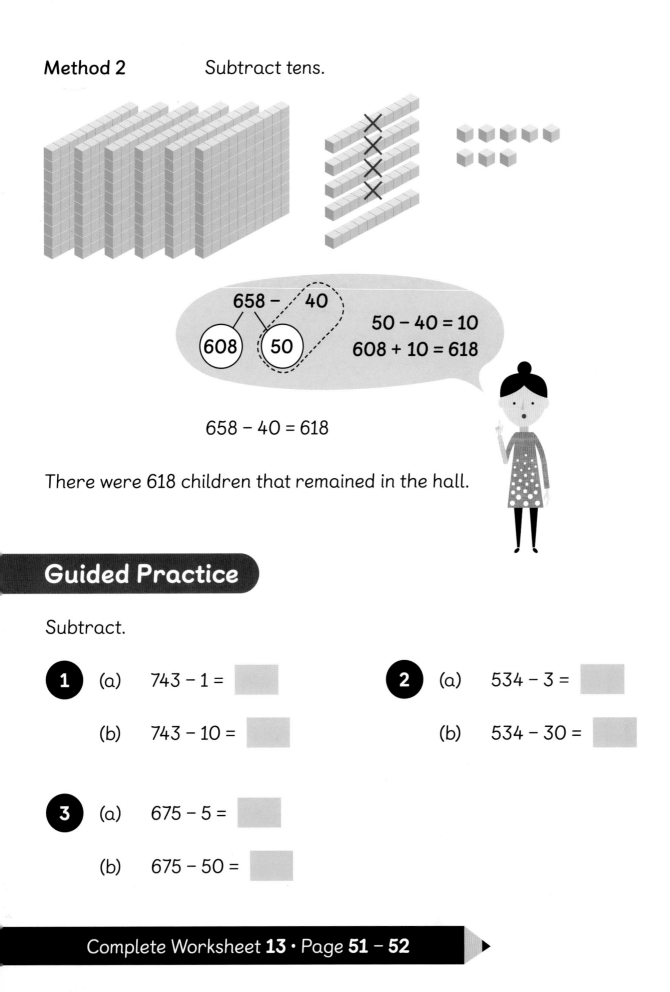

658 − 40 = 618

There were 618 children that remained in the hall.

Guided Practice

Subtract.

1 (a) 743 − 1 =

   (b) 743 − 10 =

2 (a) 534 − 3 =

   (b) 534 − 30 =

3 (a) 675 − 5 =

   (b) 675 − 50 =

Complete Worksheet 13 · Page 51 − 52

Simple Subtracting

In Focus

There were 658 children at a concert.
500 left the hall at the end of the concert.
How many children remained in the hall?

Let's Learn

Subtract 500 from 658.

Method 1   Count back in hundreds from 658.

658 − 500 = 158

658, 558, 458, 358, 258, 158

Method 2　　　　Subtract hundreds.

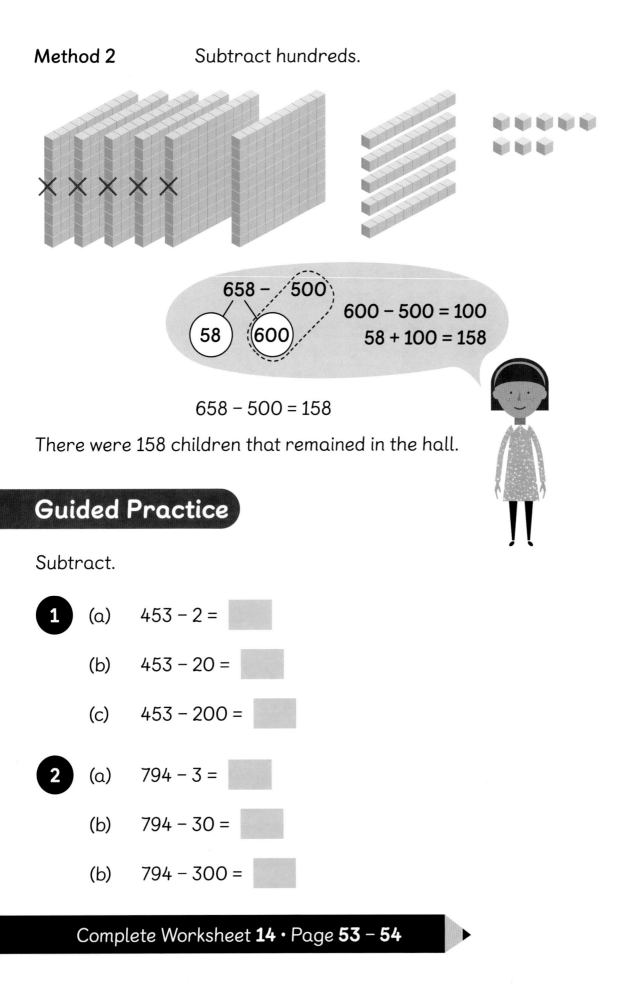

$$658 - 500 = 158$$

There were 158 children that remained in the hall.

Guided Practice

Subtract.

1　(a)　$453 - 2 = $ ⬜

　　(b)　$453 - 20 = $ ⬜

　　(c)　$453 - 200 = $ ⬜

2　(a)　$794 - 3 = $ ⬜

　　(b)　$794 - 30 = $ ⬜

　　(b)　$794 - 300 = $ ⬜

Complete Worksheet **14** · Page **53 – 54**

Simple Subtracting

In Focus

There were 975 beads in a jar.
Emma used 723 beads to make some necklaces.
How many beads were left in the jar?

Let's Learn

Subtract 723 from 975.

Step 1   Subtract the ones.
          5 ones − 3 ones = 2 ones

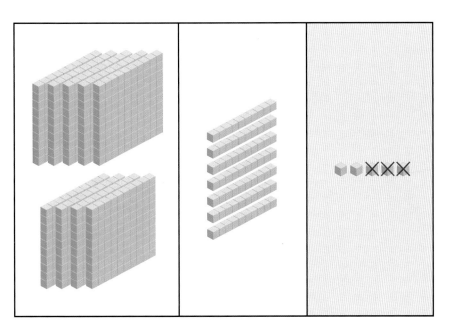

h	t	o
9	7	5
− 7	2	3
		2

Step 2   Subtract the tens.
7 tens − 2 tens = 5 tens

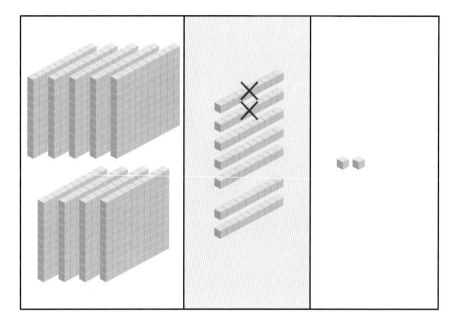

h	t	o
9	7	5
− 7	2	3
	5	2

Step 3   Subtract the hundreds.
9 hundreds − 7 hundreds = 2 hundreds

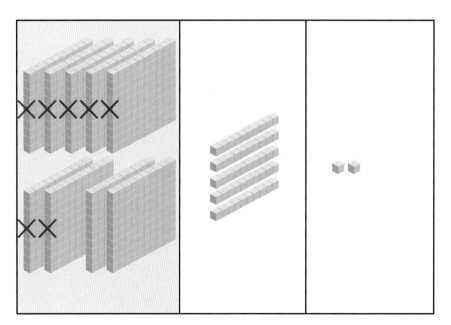

h	t	o
9	7	5
− 7	2	3
2	5	2

975 − 723 = 252

There were 252 beads left in the jar.

1 375 − 142 = ▢

$$
\begin{array}{r}
3\quad7\quad5 \\
-\quad1\quad4\quad2 \\
\hline
\boxed{}\quad\boxed{}\quad\boxed{} \\
\hline
\end{array}
$$

2 689 − 407 = ▢

$$
\begin{array}{r}
6\quad8\quad9 \\
-\quad4\quad0\quad7 \\
\hline
\boxed{}\quad\boxed{}\quad\boxed{} \\
\hline
\end{array}
$$

3 548 − 17 = ▢

4 424 − 123 = ▢

5 904 − 103 = ▢

Complete Worksheet **15** • Page **55 − 56**

Subtracting with Renaming

In Focus

1 is smaller than 6. How can I subtract 6 ones from 1 one?

How can Hannah subtract to find the answer?

Let's Learn

Subtract 26 from 831.

Step 1   Regroup 1 ten into 10 ones.
Subtract the ones.
11 ones − 6 ones = 5 ones

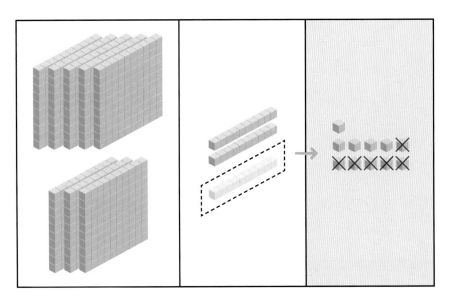

Step 2 Subtract the tens.

2 tens − 2 tens = 0 tens

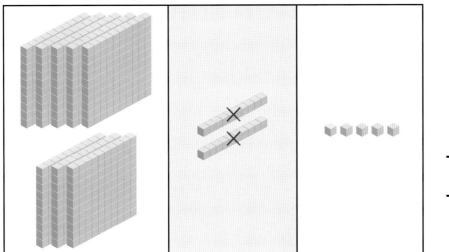

	h	t	o
	8	²3̷	¹¹1̷
−		2	6
		0	5

Step 3 Subtract the hundreds.

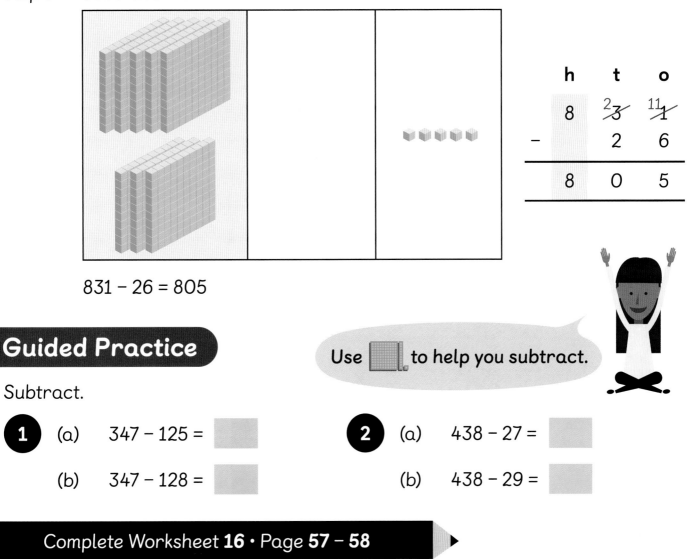

	h	t	o
	8	²3̷	¹¹1̷
−		2	6
	8	0	5

831 − 26 = 805

Guided Practice

Use 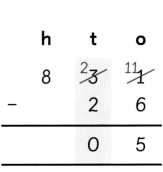 to help you subtract.

Subtract.

1 (a) 347 − 125 =

(b) 347 − 128 =

2 (a) 438 − 27 =

(b) 438 − 29 =

Complete Worksheet **16** · Page **57 – 58**

Subtracting with Renaming

In Focus

 has 608 stickers in her collection.

has 135 fewer stickers than .

What is the number of stickers that has?

Use to help you subtract.

Let's Learn

Subtract 135 from 608.

Step 1   Subtract the ones.
8 ones – 5 ones = 3 ones

608

500   100   8

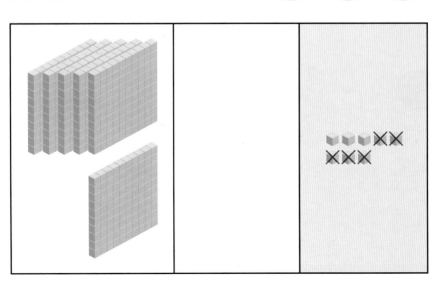

	h	t	o
	6	0	8
–	1	3	5
			3

Step 2 Regroup 1 hundred into 10 tens.
Subtract the tens.
10 tens − 3 tens = 7 tens

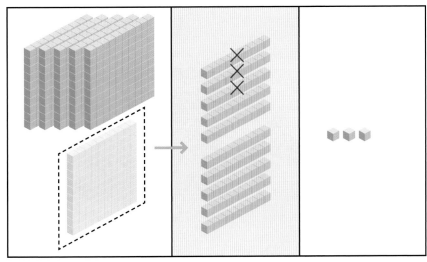

	h	t	o
	⁵6̸	¹⁰0̸	8
−	1	3	5
		7	3

Step 3 Subtract the hundreds.
5 hundreds − 1 hundred = 4 hundreds

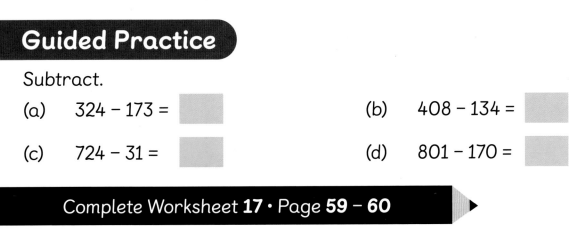

	h	t	o
	⁵6̸	¹⁰0̸	8
−	1	3	5
	4	7	3

608 − 135 = 473

Guided Practice

Subtract.

(a) 324 − 173 =

(b) 408 − 134 =

(c) 724 − 31 =

(d) 801 − 170 =

Complete Worksheet **17** · Page **59 – 60**

Subtracting with Renaming

In Focus

How can Ruby find the answer?

Let's Learn

Subtract 269 from 520.

Step 1   Regroup 1 ten into 10 ones.
Subtract the ones.
10 ones − 9 ones = 1 one

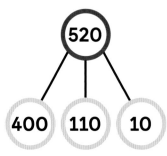

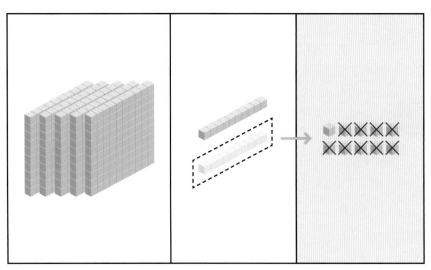

Step 2 Regroup 1 hundred into 10 tens.
Subtract the tens.
11 tens − 6 tens = 5 tens

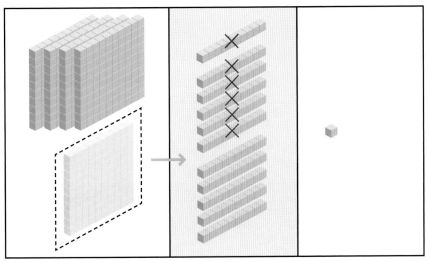

```
      h    t    o
     4     11   10
     5̸    1̸2̸   1̸0̸
  −  2     6    9
  _____
           5    1
```

Step 3 Subtract the hundreds.
4 hundreds − 2 hundreds = 2 hundreds

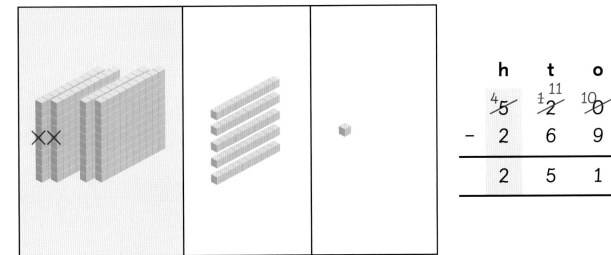

```
      h    t    o
     4     11   10
     5̸    1̸2̸   1̸0̸
  −  2     6    9
  _____
     2     5    1
```

520 − 269 = 251

Guided Practice

Subtract.

(a) 428 − 79 = [ ]

(b) 342 − 195 = [ ]

(c) 530 − 98 = [ ]

(d) 402 − 117 = [ ]

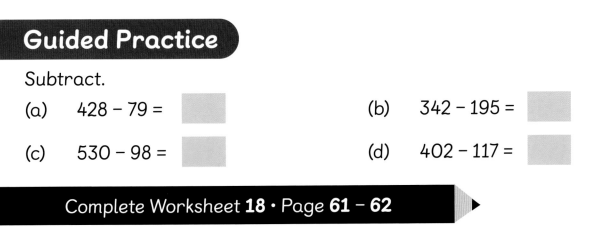

Complete Worksheet **18** · Page **61 – 62**

Subtracting with Renaming

In Focus

In a school, there are 300 pupils.
125 of them are boys.
How many girls are there?

Let's Learn

Subtract 125 from 300.

Step 1 Regroup 1 hundred into 10 tens.
Regroup 1 ten into 10 ones.
Subtract the ones.
10 ones − 5 ones = 5 ones

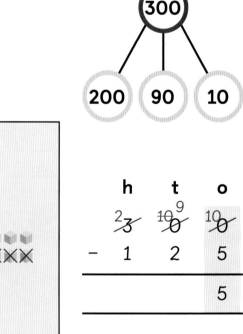

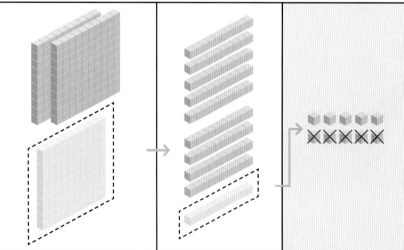

Step 2   Subtract the tens.

9 tens − 2 tens = 7 tens

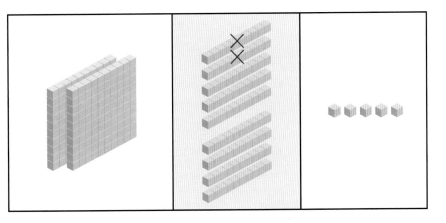

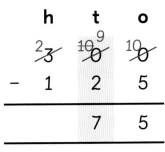

Step 3   Subtract the hundreds.

2 hundreds − 1 hundred = 1 hundred

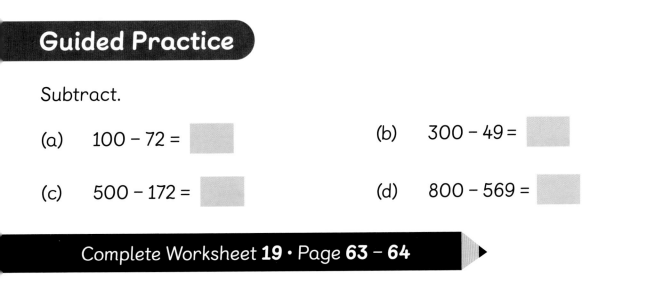

300 − 125 = 175

There are 175 girls in the school.

Guided Practice

Subtract.

(a)   100 − 72 =

(b)   300 − 49 =

(c)   500 − 172 =

(d)   800 − 569 =

Complete Worksheet 19 · Page 63 − 64

Using Models

What should we do to find the total number of pencils?

Let's Learn

1 Use 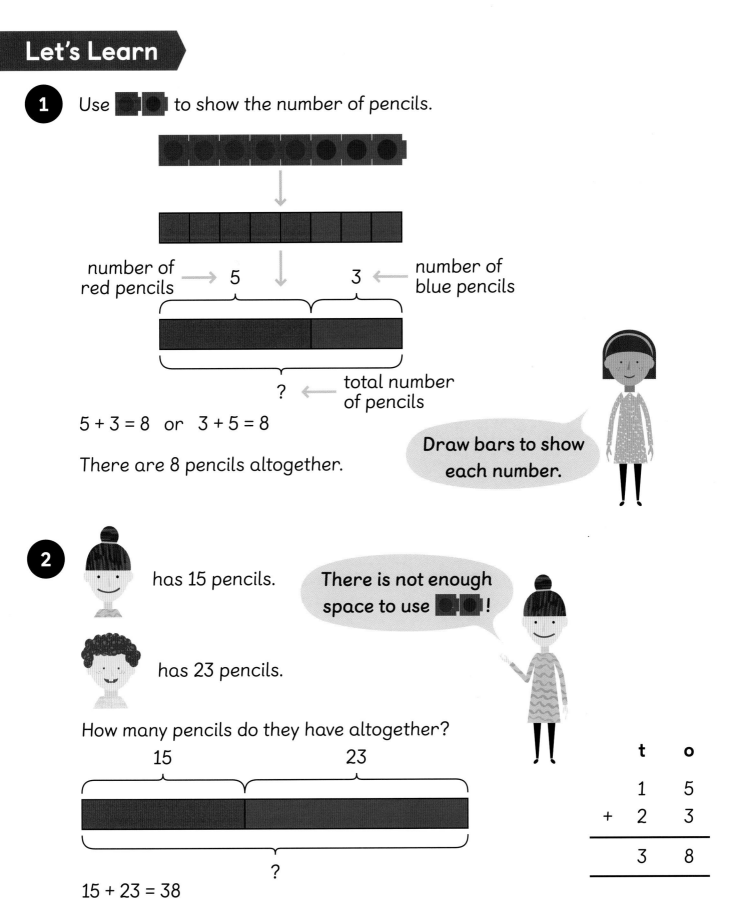 to show the number of pencils.

number of red pencils → 5   3 ← number of blue pencils

? ← total number of pencils

5 + 3 = 8   or   3 + 5 = 8

There are 8 pencils altogether.

Draw bars to show each number.

2   has 15 pencils.

There is not enough space to use ▮◉!

has 23 pencils.

How many pencils do they have altogether?

15   23

?

15 + 23 = 38

They have 38 pencils altogether.

t	o
1	5
+ 2	3
3	8

Guided Practice

Solve.

1 Sam had 45 stamps.
His father gave him 39 stamps.
How many stamps did Sam have?

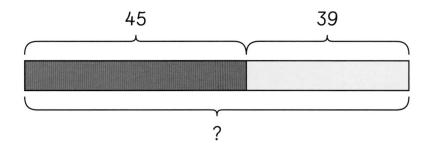

2 There are 36 children in the school band.
19 of them are boys.
How many girls are there?

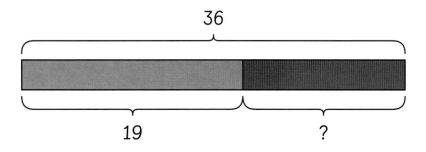

Complete Worksheet **20** • Page **65 – 66**

Using Models

In Focus

Hannah baked 400 tarts.
She gave 270 tarts away.
How many tarts did Hannah have left?

Let's Learn

Subtract 270 from 400.

400

270   ?

```
      h   t   o
      ³4̶ ¹⁰0̶  0
  -   2   7   0
  _____
      1   3   0
```

400
300   100

400 – 270 = [ ]

300 – 200 = [ ]

100 – 70 = [ ]

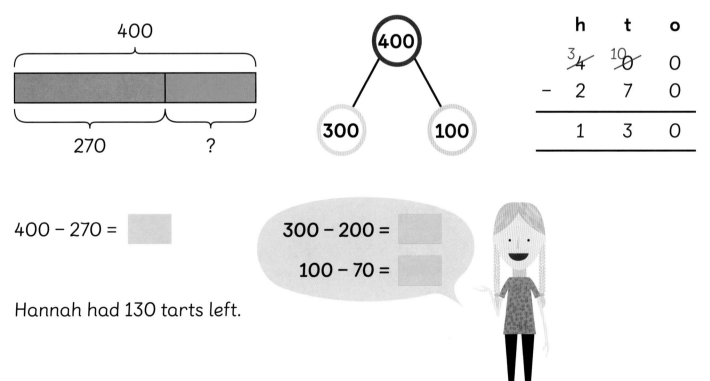

Hannah had 130 tarts left.

Solve using models.

1 There are 24 marbles in a jar.
Ravi puts 124 more marbles into the jar.
How many marbles are there in the jar now?

2 A farmer collects 127 tomatoes and 235 strawberries.
How many fruits does he collect together?

3 Lulu has 500 buttons.
She sells 201 buttons.
How many buttons does Lulu have left?

4 A postman has to deliver 358 letters.
He delivers some letters and has 289 letters left to deliver.
How many letters has he delivered?

Complete Worksheet 21 • Page 67 – 68

Using Models

In Focus

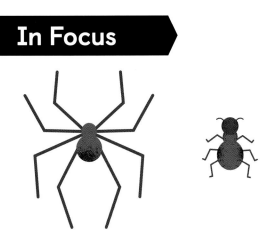

How many more legs does a spider have than an ant?

Let's Learn

1   A spider has 8 legs.
An ant has 6 legs.

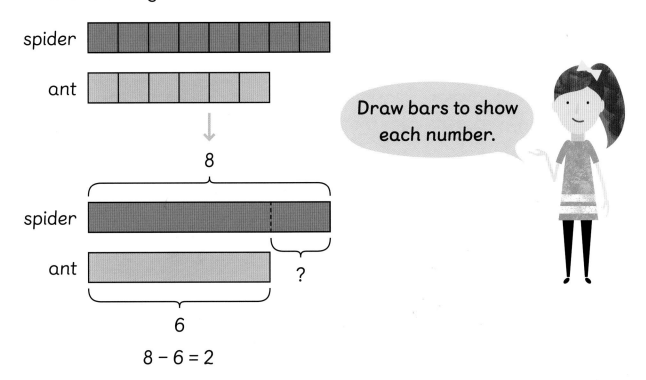

Draw bars to show each number.

$$8 - 6 = 2$$

A spider has 2 more legs than an ant.

2 Ruby has 38 stickers.
Amira has 29 stickers.
How many more stickers does Ruby have than Amira?

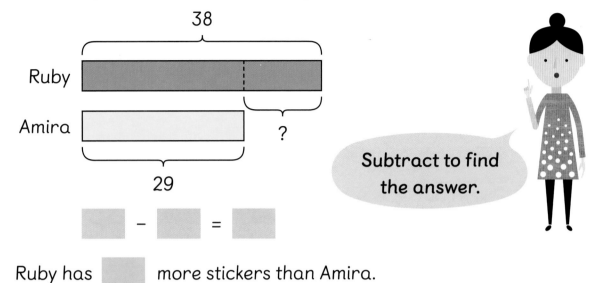

Subtract to find the answer.

Ruby has [ ] more stickers than Amira.

Guided Practice

Solve using models.

1 In a class, there are 13 boys and 19 girls.
How many more girls than boys are there?

2 Emma has 98 seashells.
Charles has 23 more seashells than Emma.
How many seashells does Charles have?

3 Elliott collects 48 pressed flowers.
He collects 16 fewer pressed flowers than Hannah.
How many pressed flowers does Hannah collect?

4 There are 71 women at a concert.
There are 29 more women than men at the concert.
How many men are there at the concert?

Complete Worksheet **22** · Page **69 – 70** ▶

Using Models

In Focus

Box A   Box B

There are 140 rubbers in Box A and 96 rubbers in Box B.
How many fewer rubbers are there in Box B than in Box A?

Let's Learn

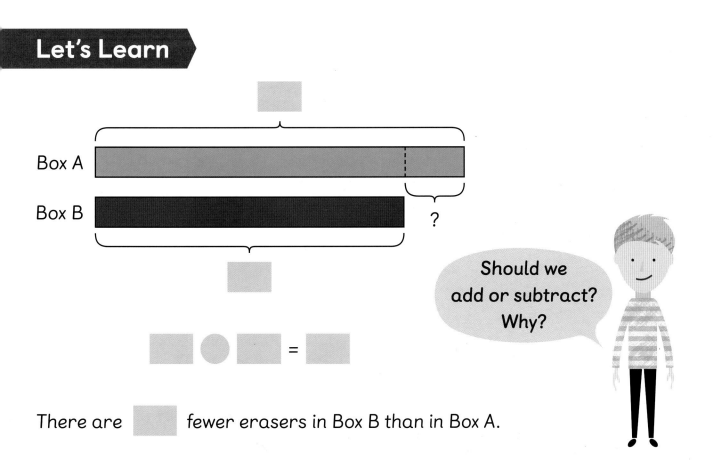

Should we add or subtract? Why?

There are ☐ fewer erasers in Box B than in Box A.

1 Ravi has 136 stamps.
Charles has 43 fewer stamps than Ravi.
How many stamps does Charles have?

Should we add or subtract?

Ravi

Charles

?

⬛ ⬤ ⬛ = ⬛

Charles has ⬛ stamps.

2 Lulu has 205 beads.
Holly has 40 more beads than Lulu.
How many beads does Holly have?

Who has more beads?

?

⬛ ⬤ ⬛ = ⬛

Should we add or subtract?

Holly has ⬛ beads.

3 Ruby folds 216 paper aeroplanes.
She folds 39 more paper aeroplanes than Elliott.
How many paper aeroplanes does Elliott fold?

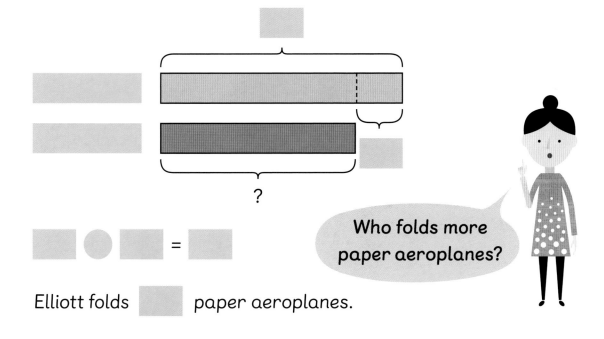

Who folds more paper aeroplanes?

Elliott folds ▢ paper aeroplanes.

Complete Worksheet **23** · Page **71 – 73** ▶

Mind Workout ▶

Some numbers are given.

Use the numbers to form two 3-digit numbers.

Subtract the numbers to get the greatest answer.

Show your work on

h	t	o
▢	▢	▢
▢	▢	▢
▢	▢	▢

Look at the subtraction equation.

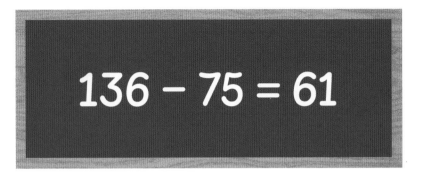

$$136 - 75 = 61$$

Write a word problem using the equation.

Show how you solve your word problem using a model.

I know how to...

☐ add numbers without renaming.

☐ add numbers with renaming.

☐ subtract numbers without renaming.

☐ subtract numbers with renaming.

☐ solve word problems involving addition and subtraction.

Self Check

What are the different ways to count
the number of flowers?

Chapter 3
Multiplication and Division

Multiplying by 3

In Focus

How many flowers are there altogether?

Let's Learn

1

 | 1 group of 3
$1 \times 3 = 3$

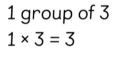

 | 2 groups of 3
$2 \times 3 = 6$

 | 3 groups of 3
$3 \times 3 = 9$

 | 4 groups of 3
$4 \times 3 = 12$

There are 12 flowers altogether.

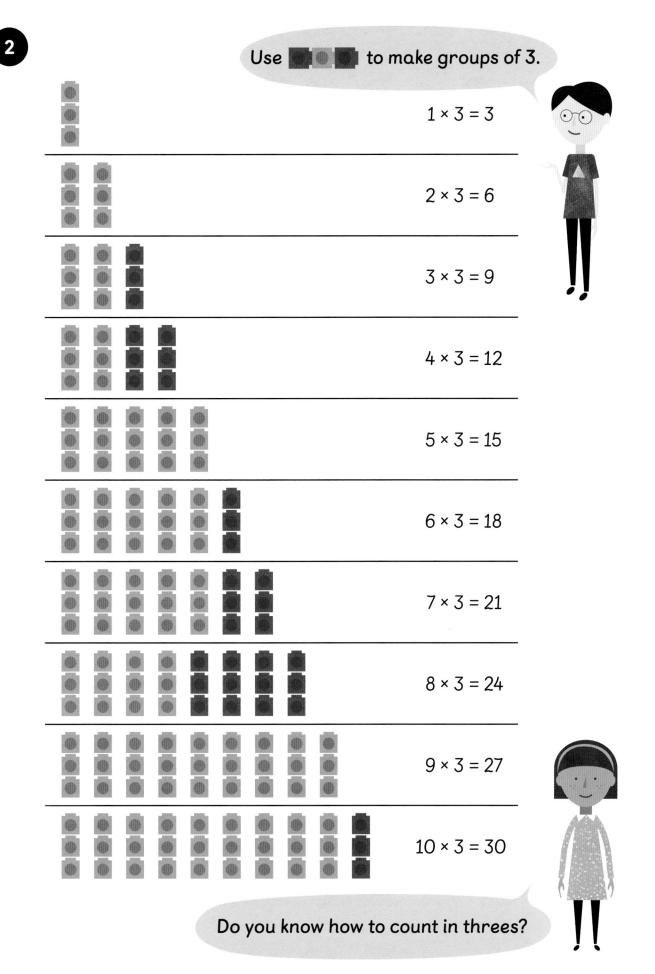

2

Use 🔲⚪🔲 to make groups of 3.

$1 \times 3 = 3$

$2 \times 3 = 6$

$3 \times 3 = 9$

$4 \times 3 = 12$

$5 \times 3 = 15$

$6 \times 3 = 18$

$7 \times 3 = 21$

$8 \times 3 = 24$

$9 \times 3 = 27$

$10 \times 3 = 30$

Do you know how to count in threes?

3 Count in threes.

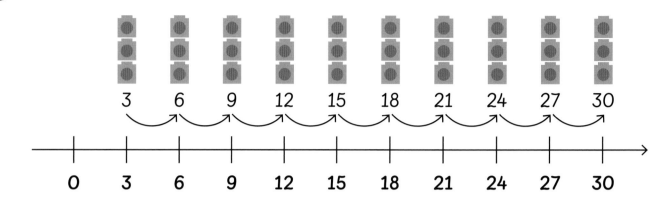

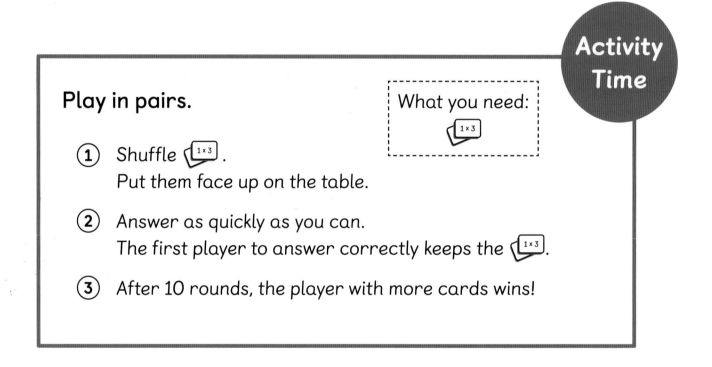

Play in pairs.

What you need:
1×3

① Shuffle 1×3 .
Put them face up on the table.

② Answer as quickly as you can.
The first player to answer correctly keeps the 1×3 .

③ After 10 rounds, the player with more cards wins!

Activity Time

Guided Practice

Write the missing numbers.

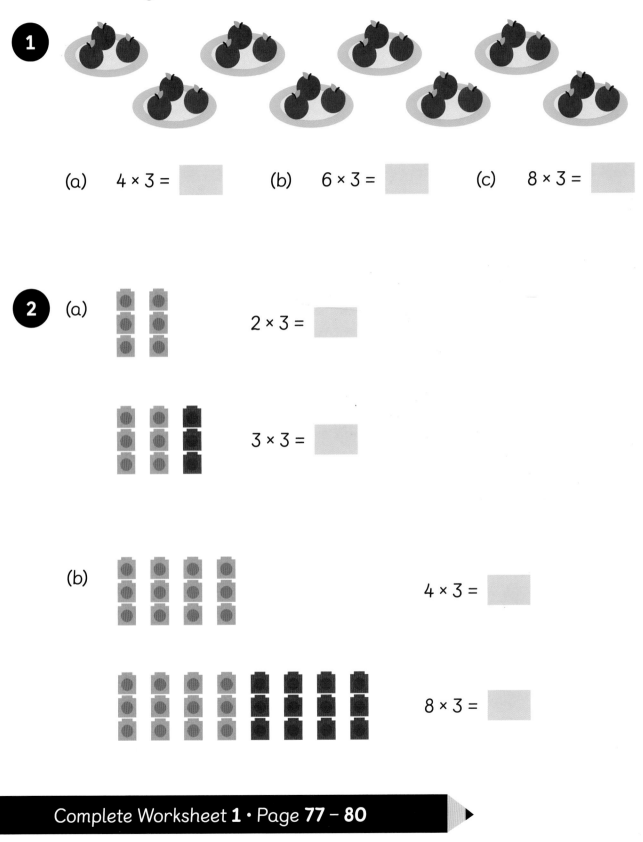

1

(a) 4 × 3 = ☐

(b) 6 × 3 = ☐

(c) 8 × 3 = ☐

2 (a)

2 × 3 = ☐

3 × 3 = ☐

(b)

4 × 3 = ☐

8 × 3 = ☐

Complete Worksheet **1** • Page **77 – 80**

Multiplying by 3

In Focus

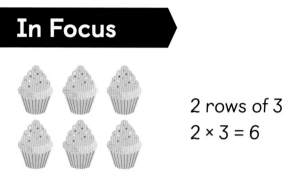

2 rows of 3
2 × 3 = 6

If we know 2 × 3 = 6, how can we tell what 3 × 3 is?

Let's Learn

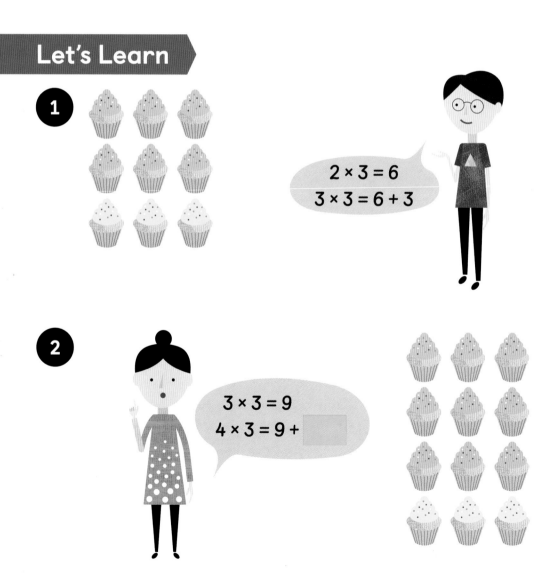

1

2 × 3 = 6
3 × 3 = 6 + 3

2

3 × 3 = 9
4 × 3 = 9 +

Write the missing numbers.

1 $5 \times 3 = 15$

$6 \times 3 = 15 +$ [ ] $=$ [ ]

2 $2 \times 3 = 6$

$4 \times 3 =$ [ ]

$8 \times 3 =$ [ ]

$9 \times 3 =$ [ ] $+ 3 =$ [ ]

3 Complete the number pattern.

3, 6, 9, 12, 15, [ ], [ ], 24, [ ], 30

Complete Worksheet **2** • Page **81 – 82**

Multiplying by 4

In Focus

How many fish are there in all?

Let's Learn

1 1 bowl has 4 fish.

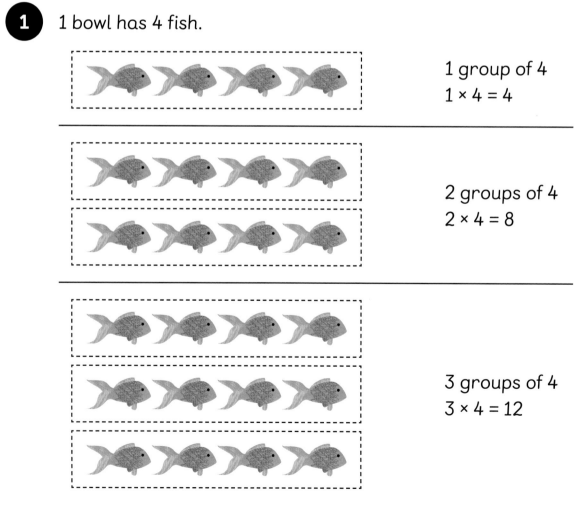

1 group of 4
$1 \times 4 = 4$

2 groups of 4
$2 \times 4 = 8$

3 groups of 4
$3 \times 4 = 12$

There are 12 fish in all.

2

Use to make groups of 4.

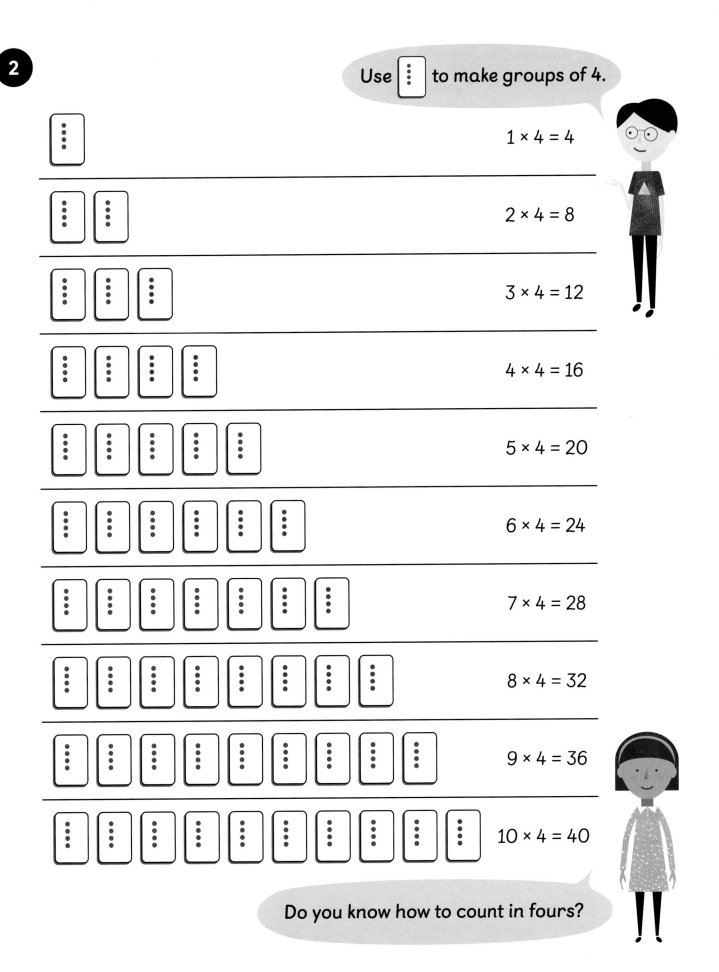

$1 \times 4 = 4$

$2 \times 4 = 8$

$3 \times 4 = 12$

$4 \times 4 = 16$

$5 \times 4 = 20$

$6 \times 4 = 24$

$7 \times 4 = 28$

$8 \times 4 = 32$

$9 \times 4 = 36$

$10 \times 4 = 40$

Do you know how to count in fours?

Guided Practice

Write the missing numbers.

1

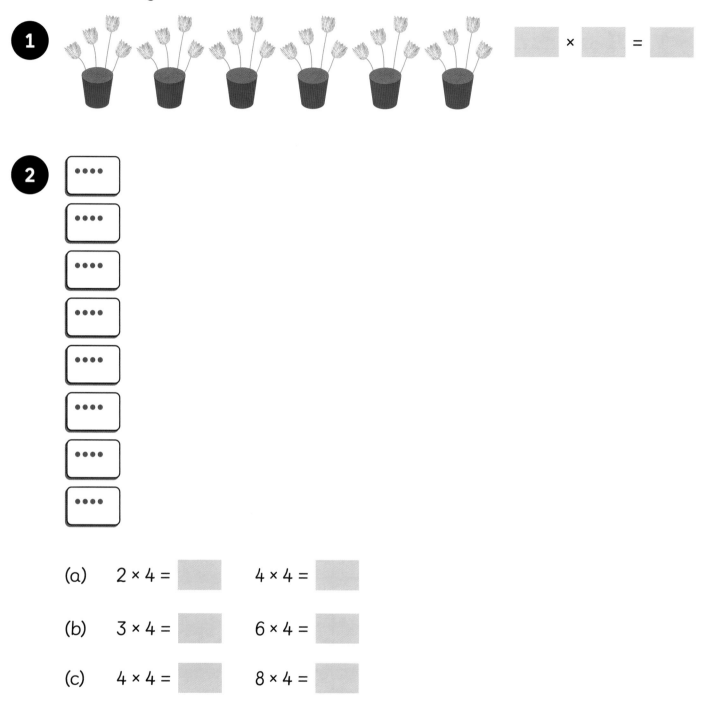

$$\boxed{} \times \boxed{} = \boxed{}$$

2

(a) $2 \times 4 = \boxed{}$ $4 \times 4 = \boxed{}$

(b) $3 \times 4 = \boxed{}$ $6 \times 4 = \boxed{}$

(c) $4 \times 4 = \boxed{}$ $8 \times 4 = \boxed{}$

Complete Worksheet 3 · Page 83 – 86

Multiplying by 4

In Focus

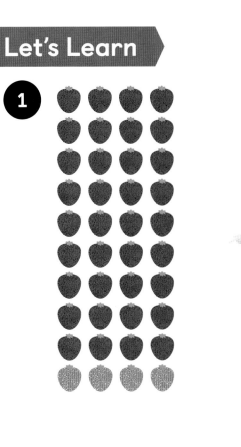

10 rows of 4 = 40
$10 \times 4 = 40$

$10 \times 4 = 40$
What is 9×4?
How can we tell?

Let's Learn

1

$9 \times 4 = 40 - \boxed{} = \boxed{}$

2

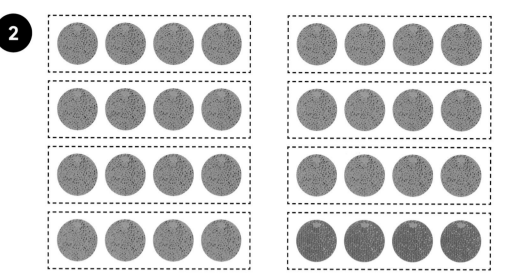

$2 \times 4 = 8$

$4 \times 4 = 16$

$8 \times 4 = 32$

$7 \times 4 = 32 - \boxed{} = \boxed{}$

3

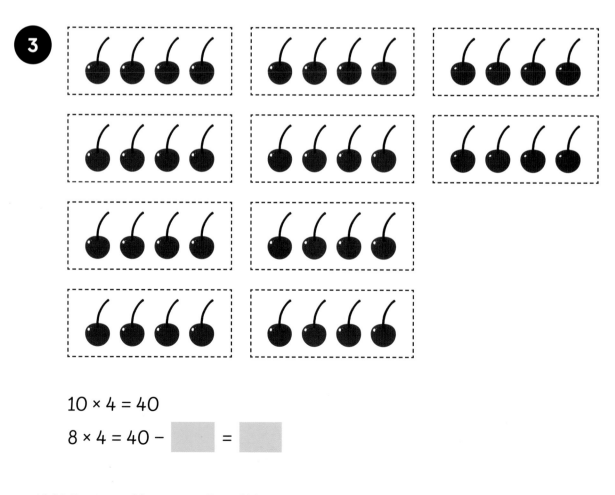

$10 \times 4 = 40$

$8 \times 4 = 40 - \boxed{} = \boxed{}$

Write the missing numbers.

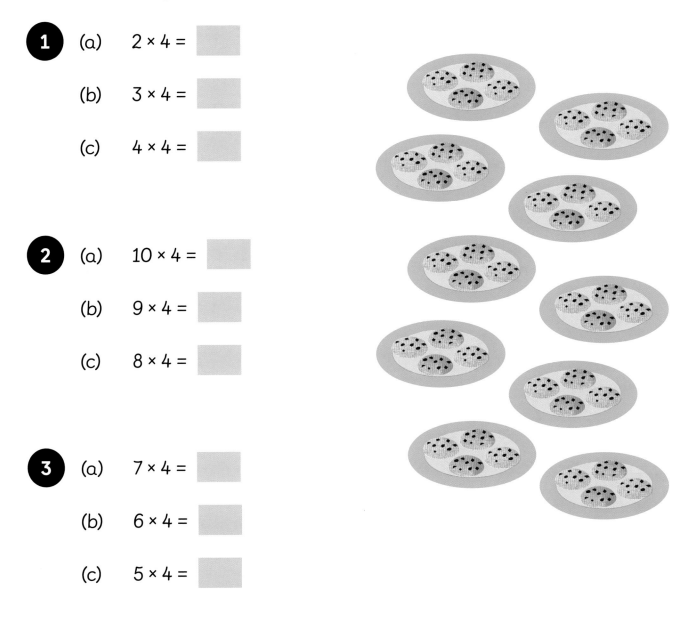

1 (a) 2 × 4 = ☐

(b) 3 × 4 = ☐

(c) 4 × 4 = ☐

2 (a) 10 × 4 = ☐

(b) 9 × 4 = ☐

(c) 8 × 4 = ☐

3 (a) 7 × 4 = ☐

(b) 6 × 4 = ☐

(c) 5 × 4 = ☐

Complete Worksheet **4** • Page **87 – 88**

Multiplying by 4 and 8

In Focus

How many  are there?
How can we tell?

Let's Learn

1

$1 \times 4 = 4$

$1 \times 8 = 8$

$$2 \times 4 = 8$$

$$2 \times 8 = 16$$

$$3 \times 4 = 12$$

$$3 \times 8 = 24$$

2

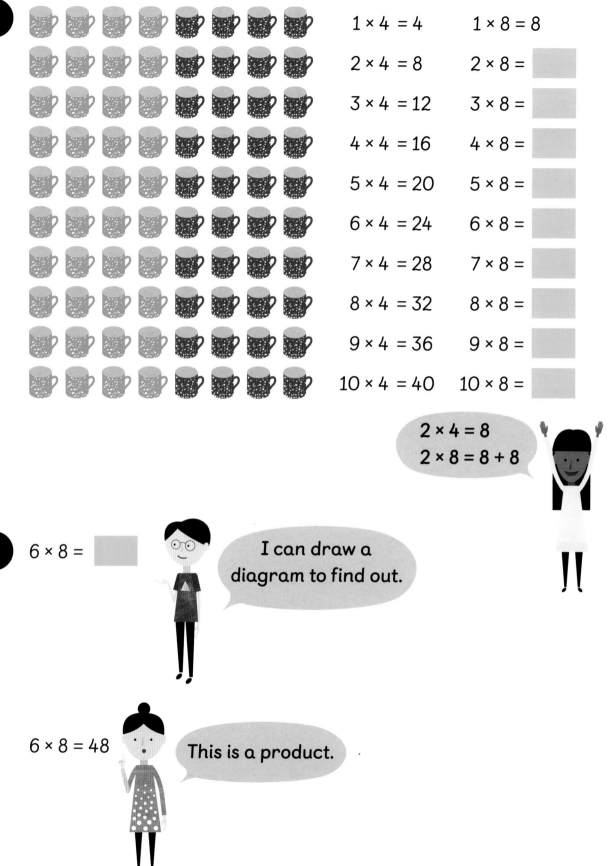

$1 \times 4 = 4$	$1 \times 8 = 8$
$2 \times 4 = 8$	$2 \times 8 = $
$3 \times 4 = 12$	$3 \times 8 = $
$4 \times 4 = 16$	$4 \times 8 = $
$5 \times 4 = 20$	$5 \times 8 = $
$6 \times 4 = 24$	$6 \times 8 = $
$7 \times 4 = 28$	$7 \times 8 = $
$8 \times 4 = 32$	$8 \times 8 = $
$9 \times 4 = 36$	$9 \times 8 = $
$10 \times 4 = 40$	$10 \times 8 = $

$2 \times 4 = 8$
$2 \times 8 = 8 + 8$

3 $6 \times 8 = $

I can draw a diagram to find out.

$6 \times 8 = 48$

This is a product.

We say that the product of 6 and 8 is 48.

Write the missing numbers.

1 (a)   3 × 4 = ▢

   3 × 8 = ▢

(b)   5 × 4 = ▢

   5 × 8 = ▢

(c)   2 × 8 = ▢

   3 × 8 = ▢

(d)   2 × 8 = ▢

   5 × 8 = ▢

   7 × 8 = ▢

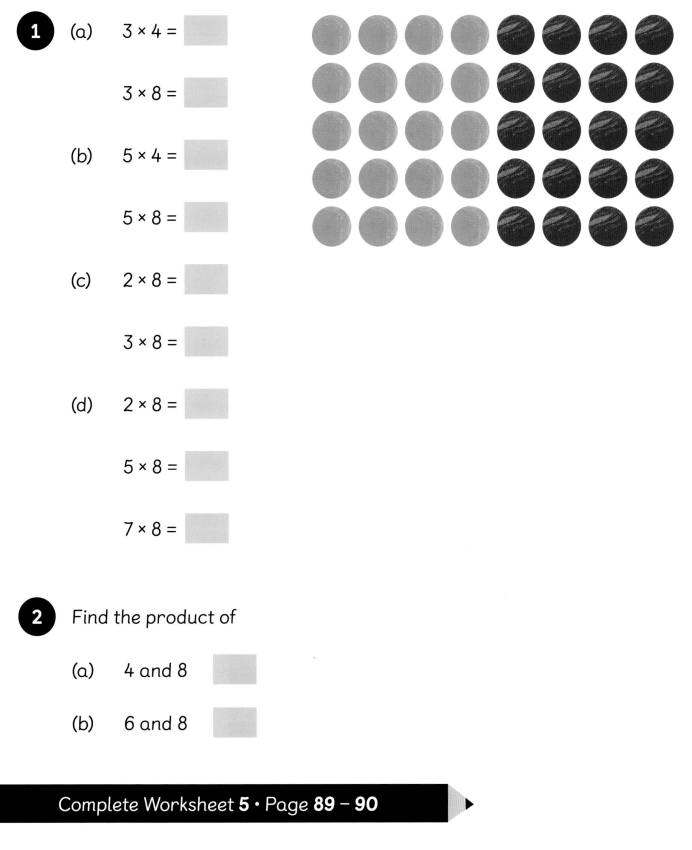

2 Find the product of

(a)   4 and 8   ▢

(b)   6 and 8   ▢

Complete Worksheet **5** • Page **89 – 90**

Multiplying by 8

In Focus

How many children are there?

Let's Learn

1

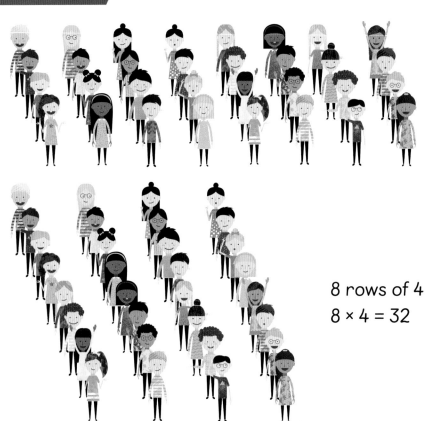

4 rows of 8
4 × 8 = 32

8 rows of 4
8 × 4 = 32

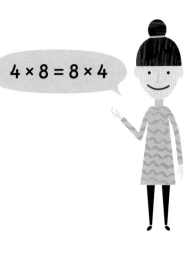

$4 × 8 = 8 × 4$

2

2 × 4 is the same as 4 × 2 = 8.

Activity Time

Work in groups of 4.

What you need:

① Make three multiplication stories.

Draw pictures to show your stories.

Example

There are 2 trays.

Each tray has 8 cookies.

2 × 8 = 16

There are 16 cookies in all.

② Use ⬤ to show how you multiply.

Guided Practice

Find the product of the following.

(a)   3 and 4 _____   4 and 3 _____

(b)   3 and 8 _____   8 and 3 _____

Complete Worksheet 6 · Page 91 – 92

Multiplying by 8

In Focus

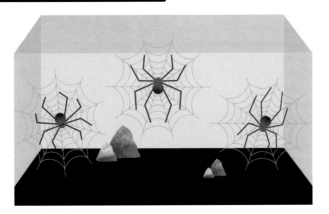

How many legs do the spiders have in all?

Let's Learn

1 Each spider has 8 legs.

1 group of 8
$1 \times 8 = 8$

2 groups of 8
$2 \times 8 = 16$

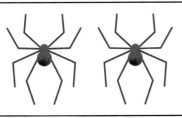

3 groups of 8
$3 \times 8 = 24$

The spiders have 24 legs in all.

2 Count in eights.

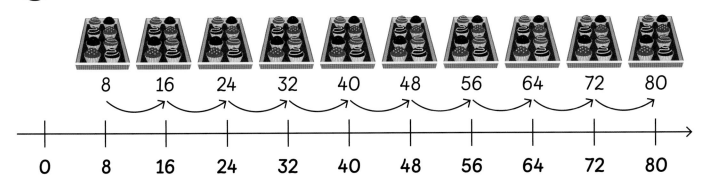

8   16   24   32   40   48   56   64   72   80

```
  +----+----+----+----+----+----+----+----+----+
0    8   16   24   32   40   48   56   64   72   80
```

3

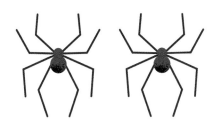

$2 \times 8 = $ ☐

$2 \times 4 = $ ☐

$2 \times 2 = $ ☐

$2 \times 0 = $ ☐

1 An octopus has 8 tentacles.
How many tentacles are there altogether on 5 octopuses?

$\boxed{} \times \boxed{} = \boxed{}$

There are $\boxed{}$ tentacles altogether on 5 octopuses.

2 Complete the 8 times table.

$1 \times 8 = \boxed{}$

$2 \times 8 = \boxed{}$ $4 \times 8 = \boxed{}$

$3 \times 8 = \boxed{}$ $6 \times 8 = \boxed{}$

$5 \times 8 = \boxed{}$ $10 \times 8 = \boxed{}$

3 Write the missing numbers.

(a) $3 \times 8 = \boxed{}$ (b) $2 \times 8 = \boxed{}$

     $5 \times 8 = \boxed{}$ $4 \times 8 = \boxed{}$

     $7 \times 8 = \boxed{}$ $8 \times 8 = \boxed{}$

4 Complete the number pattern.

8, 16, 24, $\boxed{}$, 40, $\boxed{}$, 56, $\boxed{}$, 72, $\boxed{}$

Complete Worksheet 7 • Page 93 – 94

Dividing by 3

In Focus

Each stand can hold 3 birds.
At least how many stands are needed?

Let's Learn

1 Put the birds in groups of 3.

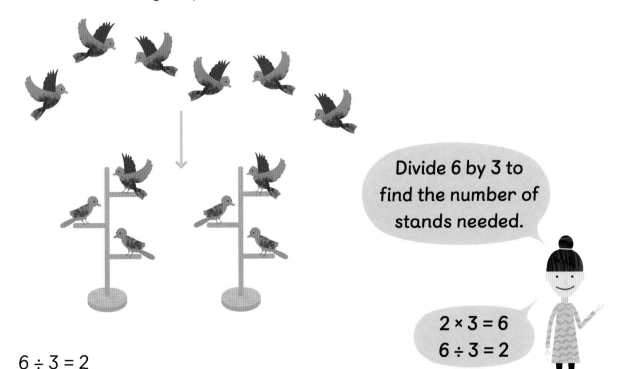

Divide 6 by 3 to find the number of stands needed.

2 × 3 = 6
6 ÷ 3 = 2

6 ÷ 3 = 2

At least 2 stands are needed.

2 Put 6 birds into 3 equal groups.

$6 \div 3 = 2$

There are 2 birds on each stand.

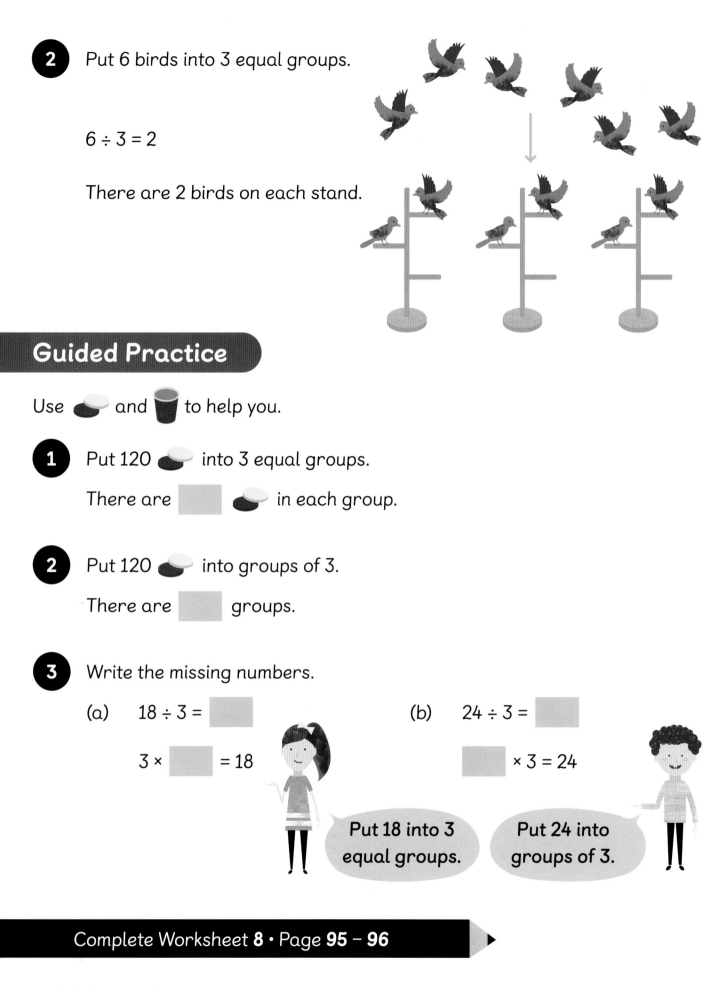

Guided Practice

Use and to help you.

1 Put 120 into 3 equal groups.

There are ☐ in each group.

2 Put 120 into groups of 3.

There are ☐ groups.

3 Write the missing numbers.

(a) $18 \div 3 = $ ☐

$3 \times$ ☐ $= 18$

Put 18 into 3 equal groups.

(b) $24 \div 3 = $ ☐

☐ $\times 3 = 24$

Put 24 into groups of 3.

Complete Worksheet **8** • Page **95 – 96**

Dividing by 4

In Focus

Put these equally into 4 boxes.

How many 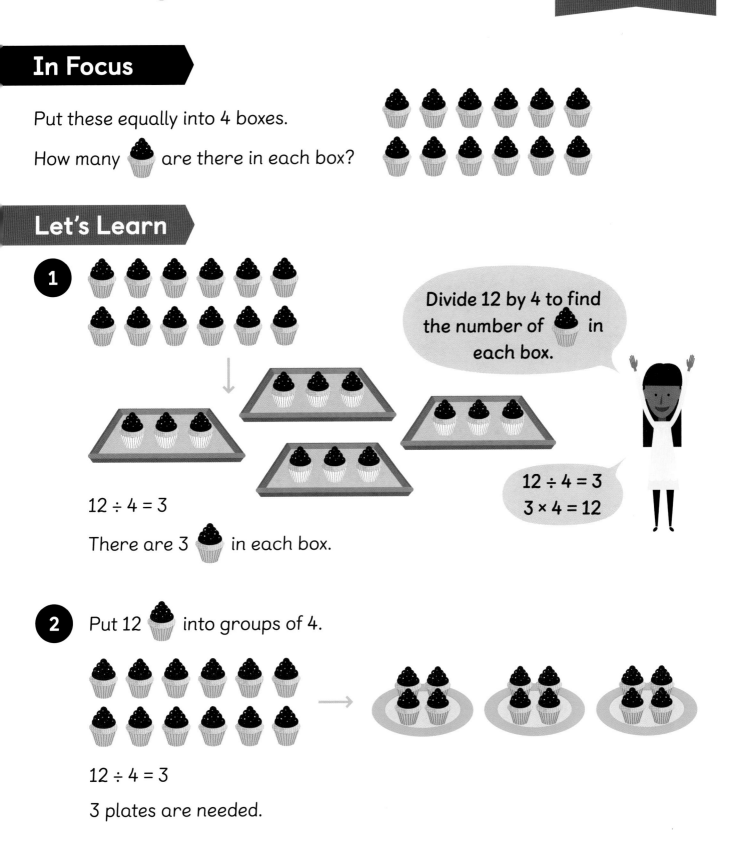 are there in each box?

Let's Learn

1

Divide 12 by 4 to find the number of in each box.

$12 \div 4 = 3$

There are 3 in each box.

$12 \div 4 = 3$
$3 \times 4 = 12$

2 Put 12 into groups of 4.

$12 \div 4 = 3$

3 plates are needed.

Guided Practice

Use 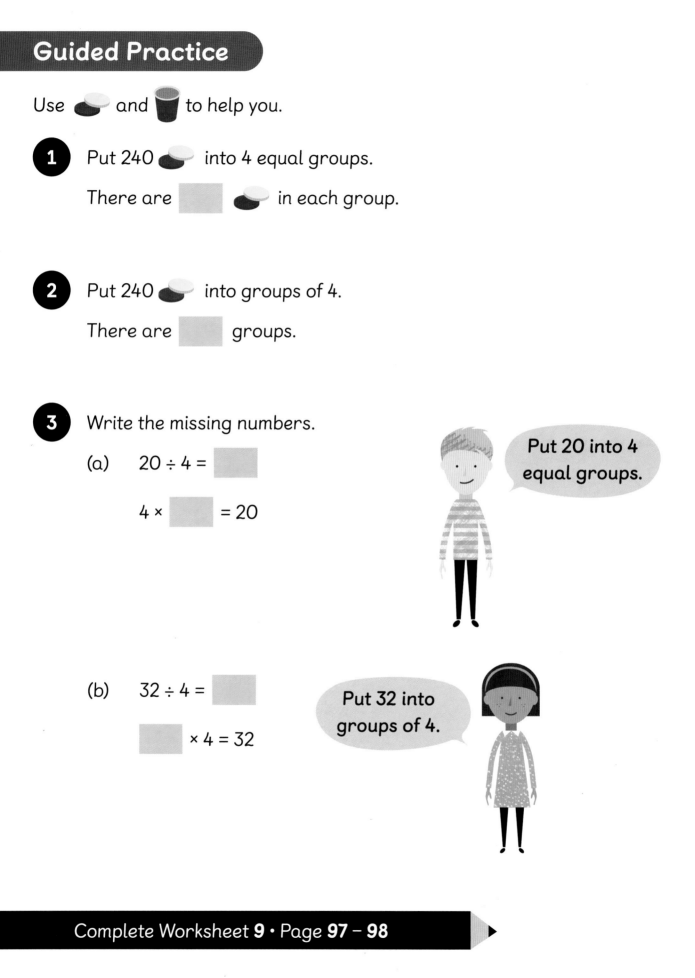 and ⬛ to help you.

1 Put 240 🍪 into 4 equal groups.

There are ⬜ 🍪 in each group.

2 Put 240 🍪 into groups of 4.

There are ⬜ groups.

3 Write the missing numbers.

(a)   20 ÷ 4 = ⬜

   4 × ⬜ = 20

> Put 20 into 4 equal groups.

(b)   32 ÷ 4 = ⬜

   ⬜ × 4 = 32

> Put 32 into groups of 4.

Complete Worksheet **9** • Page **97 – 98**

Multiplying and Dividing

In Focus

Put 4 or 5 cherries on each cake.

Can we make a family of multiplication and division equations?

Let's Learn

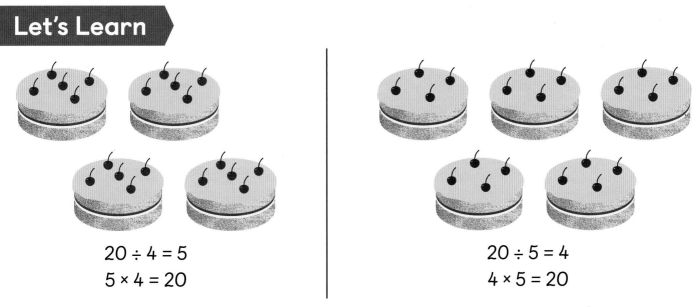

$20 \div 4 = 5$
$5 \times 4 = 20$

$20 \div 5 = 4$
$4 \times 5 = 20$

We can make a family of multiplication and division equations.

Work in pairs.

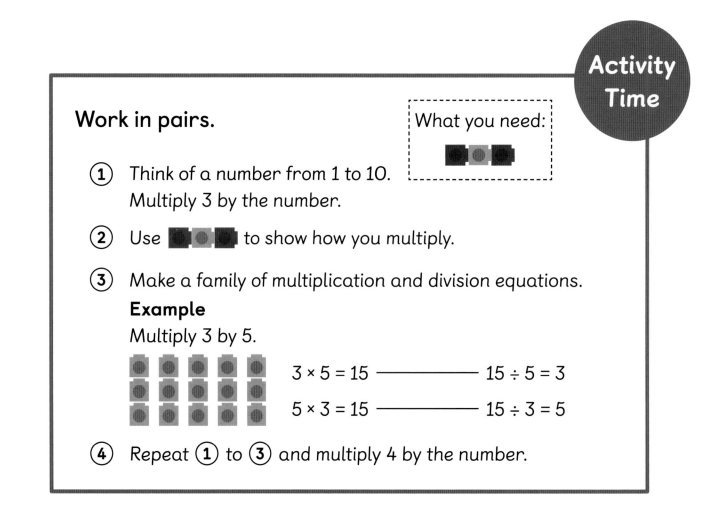

What you need:

(1) Think of a number from 1 to 10.
Multiply 3 by the number.

(2) Use ▪◦▪ to show how you multiply.

(3) Make a family of multiplication and division equations.
Example
Multiply 3 by 5.

$3 \times 5 = 15$ ——————— $15 \div 5 = 3$

$5 \times 3 = 15$ ——————— $15 \div 3 = 5$

(4) Repeat (1) to (3) and multiply 4 by the number.

Guided Practice

Make a family of multiplication and division facts.

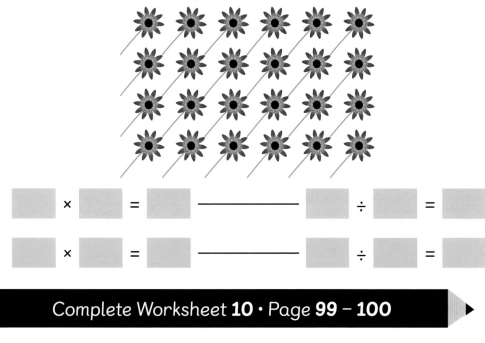

☐ × ☐ = ☐ ——————— ☐ ÷ ☐ = ☐

☐ × ☐ = ☐ ——————— ☐ ÷ ☐ = ☐

Complete Worksheet 10 · Page 99 – 100 ▶

Dividing by 4 and 8

In Focus

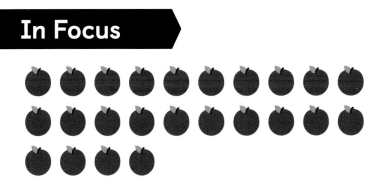

How do we put these apples into 4 and 8 equal groups?

Let's Learn

1 Put 24 apples into 4 equal groups.

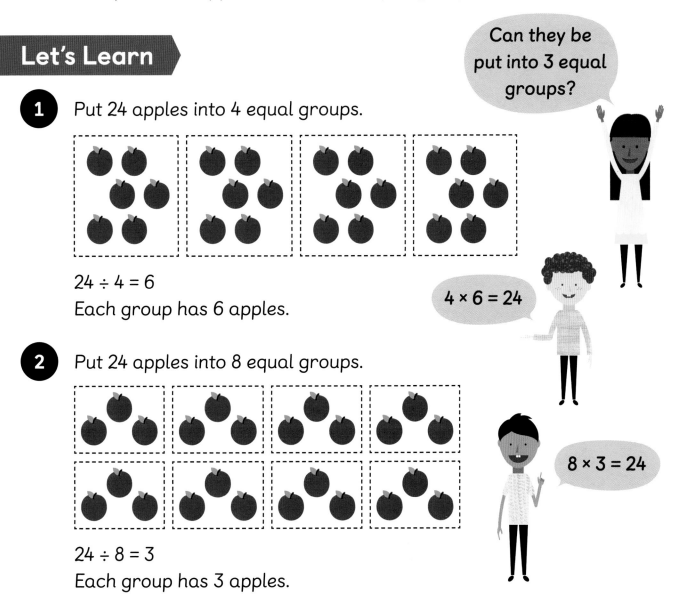

Can they be put into 3 equal groups?

$24 \div 4 = 6$
Each group has 6 apples.

$4 \times 6 = 24$

2 Put 24 apples into 8 equal groups.

$8 \times 3 = 24$

$24 \div 8 = 3$
Each group has 3 apples.

Write the missing numbers.

1

16 ÷ 4 = ☐

16 ÷ 8 = ☐

2

40 ÷ 4 = ☐

40 ÷ 8 = ☐

40 ÷ 2 = ☐

3 (a)   28 ÷ 4 = ☐   ☐ × 4 = 28

   (b)   48 ÷ 8 = ☐   ☐ × 8 = 48

   (c)   24 ÷ 8 = ☐   ☐ × 8 = 24

          24 ÷ 4 = ☐   ☐ × 4 = 24

          24 ÷ 3 = ☐   ☐ × 3 = 24

Complete Worksheet 11 · Page 101 – 102

Solving Word Problems

In Focus

How many pupils are there altogether?

Let's Learn

1 There are 4 pupils in each row.

There are 7 groups.

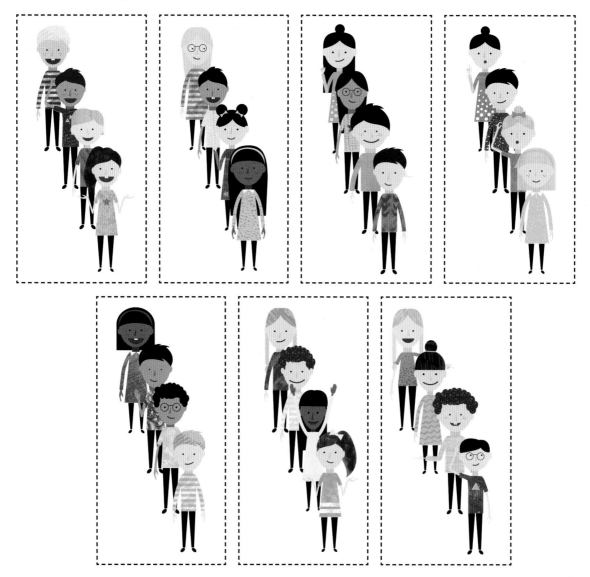

$7 \times 4 = 28$

There are 28 pupils altogether.

2　There are 5 groups of 3 children.
Each group has 3 children.
How many children are there altogether?

$5 \times 3 = 15$

There are 5 groups of 3.

There are 15 children altogether.

Solve.

 1 At a shop, toy robots are sold in sets of 3.
How many toy robots are there in 9 sets?

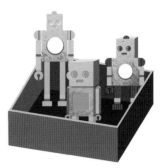

 × ☐ = ☐

 2 There are 6 shirts.
Each shirt has 4 buttons.
How many buttons are there altogether?

 × ☐ = ☐

 3 One flower has 4 petals.
How many petals do 8 flowers have?

4 There are 8 stools.
Each stool has 3 legs.
How many legs are there altogether?

Complete Worksheet 12 · Page 103 – 104

Solving Word Problems

In Focus

How many sweets are there altogether?
How many bags of sweets can Amira pack?

Should we multiply or divide to find each answer?

Let's Learn

1. Put the sweets in groups of 3.
    Multiply to find the total number of sweets.

    There are 3 sweets in each group.
    There are 8 groups.

    Multiply 3 by 8.

    We can also write 3 × 8 = 24.

    8 × 3 = 24

    There are 24 sweets altogether.

Each bag has 3 sweets.
Divide to find the number of bags of sweets.

There are 24 sweets altogether.
Amira packs 3 sweets in each bag.

$24 \div 3 = 8$

Amira can pack 8 bags of sweets.

Divide 24 by 3.

2 There are 4 children.
They share 24 slices of pizza equally.
How many slices of pizza does each child get?

Should we multiply or divide?

☐ ● ☐ = ☐

Each child gets ☐ slices of pizza.

Work in groups of 4.

What you need:

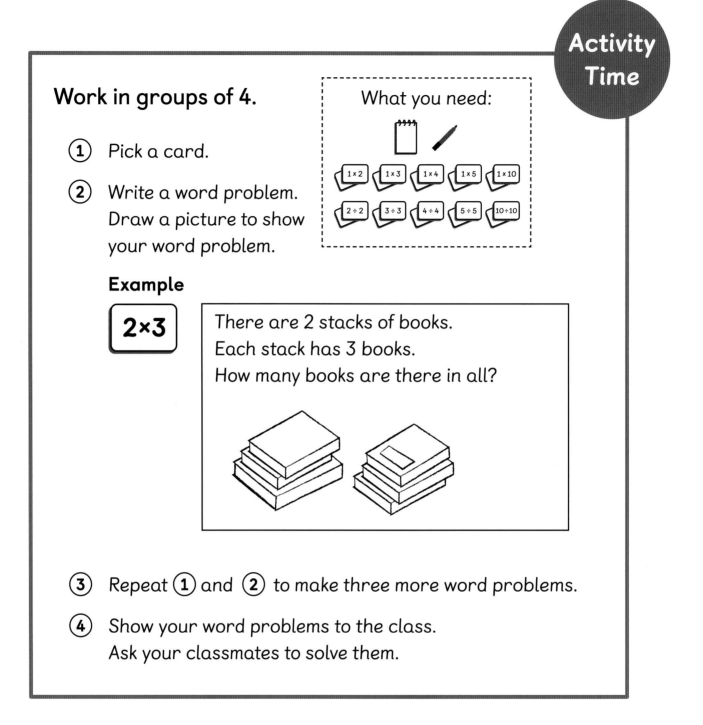

① Pick a card.

② Write a word problem.
Draw a picture to show
your word problem.

Example

2×3

There are 2 stacks of books.
Each stack has 3 books.
How many books are there in all?

③ Repeat ① and ② to make three more word problems.

④ Show your word problems to the class.
Ask your classmates to solve them.

Solve.

1 There are 3 postcards in one packet.
How many postcards are there in 8 identical packets?

2 Charles has to arrange 32 chairs in rows.
Each row has 8 chairs.
How many rows are there?

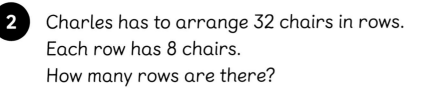

3 Sam has 8 sheets of paper.
He cuts each sheet into 4 rectangles.
How many rectangles does Sam get altogether?

Complete Worksheet 13 · Page 105 – 106

Solving Word Problems

Lesson 14

In Focus

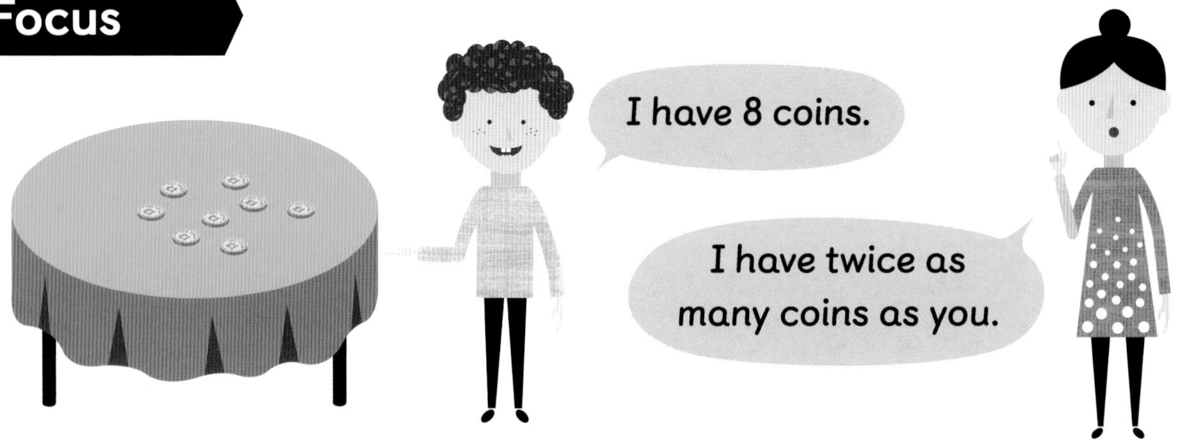

I have 8 coins.
I have twice as many coins as you.

How many coins does 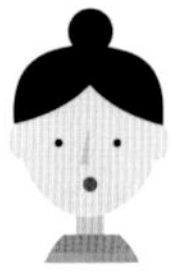 have?

Let's Learn

1

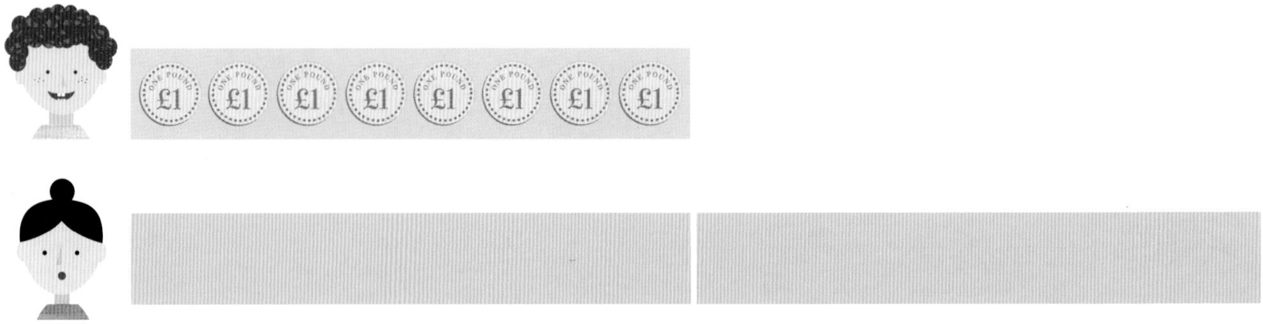

£1 £1 £1 £1 £1 £1 £1 £1

Method 1 $8 + 8 = 16$

Method 2 $2 \times 8 = 16$

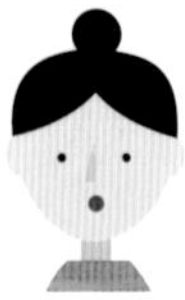 has 16 coins.

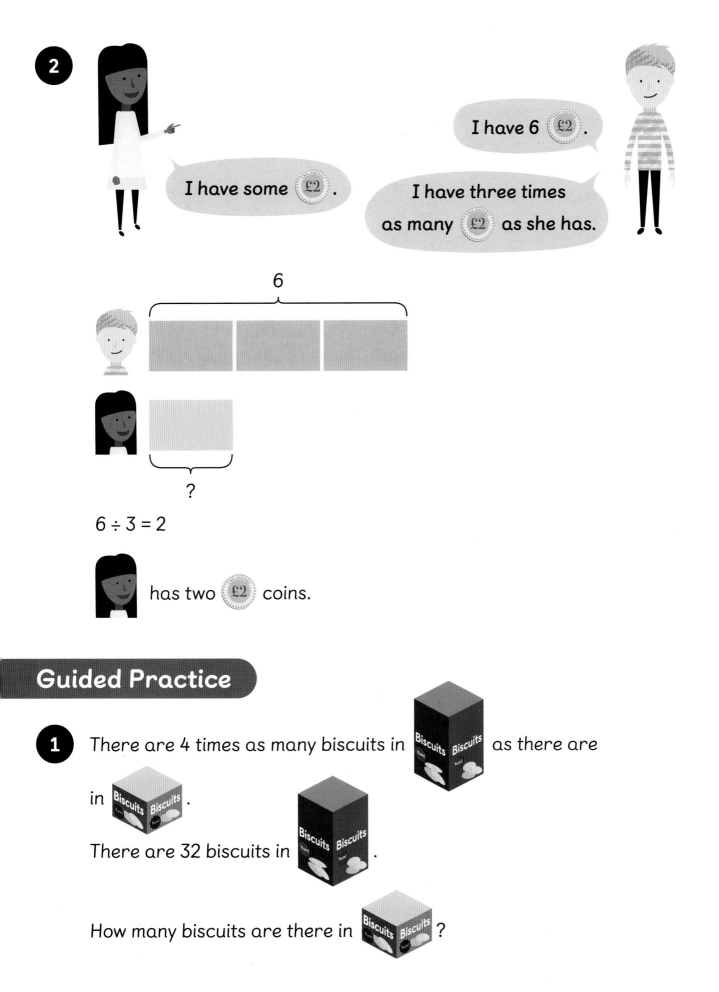

2

I have some £2.

I have 6 £2.

I have three times as many £2 as she has.

6

?

6 ÷ 3 = 2

has two £2 coins.

Guided Practice

1 There are 4 times as many biscuits in [Biscuits] as there are in [Biscuits].

There are 32 biscuits in [Biscuits].

How many biscuits are there in [Biscuits]?

2

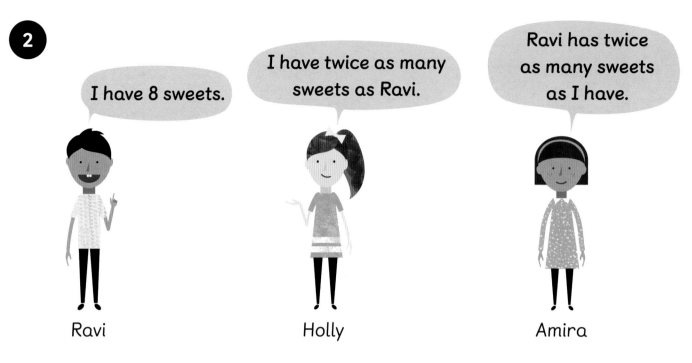

How many sweets does each child have?

3 There are 5 times as many boys as there are girls at a camp.
There are 8 girls at the camp.
How many children are there at the camp?

Complete Worksheet **14** • Page **107 – 108**

Solving Problems

In Focus

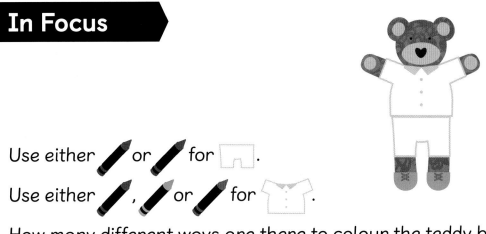

Use either ✏ or ✏ for ▢ .

Use either ✏ , ✏ or ✏ for 👕 .

How many different ways are there to colour the teddy bear's outfit?

Let's Learn

There are 2 ways to colour the ▢ .

There are 6 different ways in all.

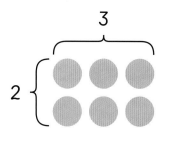

$2 \times 3 = 6$

Guided Practice

 1 Pick a fruit and a pastry.

How many different ways are there to pick a fruit and a pastry?

2 Pick a shape.

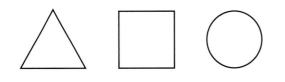

Pick a colour. Colour the shape.

How many different coloured shapes can we get?

Complete Worksheet **15** · Page **109**

Mind Workout

There are 6 figures in a pattern.
The last four figures in the pattern are shown below.

?

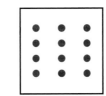

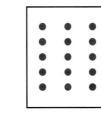

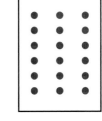

Figure 1   Figure 3   Figure 4   Figure 5   Figure 6

How many dots are there in Figure 1?

Draw to help you find out.

Look at the chart.

1	2	3	4	5	6	7	8	9	10
11	12	13	14	15	16	17	18	19	20
21	22	23	24	25	26	27	28	29	30
31	32	33	34	35	36	37	38	39	40

1 Count in twos and circle the numbers in red.

2 Count in threes and circle the numbers in orange.

3 Count in fours and circle the numbers in purple.

4 Count in fives and circle the numbers in blue.

5 Count in tens and circle the numbers in green.

Which numbers can be divided by both 3 and 4? What do you notice about the numbers?

Self Check

I know how to...

☐ do my 3 times table.

☐ do my 4 times table.

☐ do my 8 times table.

☐ divide a number by 3.

☐ divide a number by 4.

☐ divide a number by 8.

☐ solve word problems involving the 3, 4 and 8 times tables.

☐ solve word problems involving the division of 3, 4 and 8.

How many oranges are there altogether?

Chapter 4
Further Multiplication and Division

Multiplying 2-Digit Numbers

In Focus

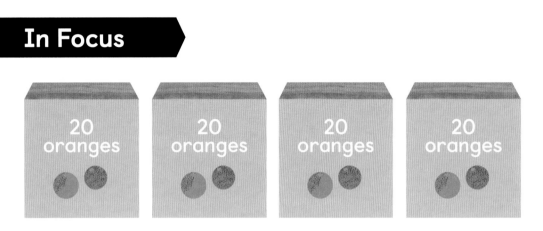

How many oranges are there in the 4 boxes altogether?

Let's Learn

1

Multiply 2 ones by 4
$2 \times 4 = 8$

```
      o
      2
×     4
──────
      8
```

2

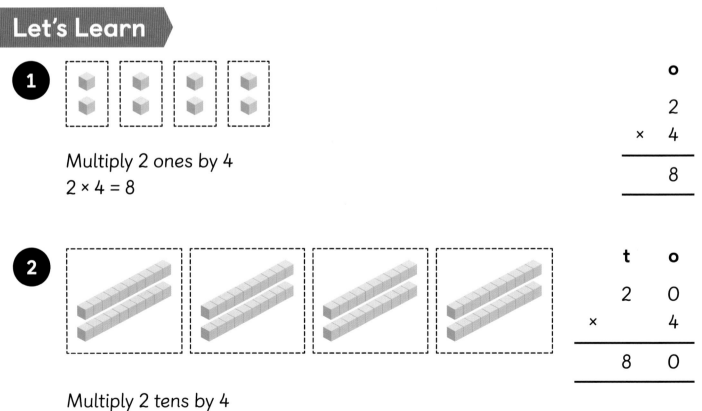

Multiply 2 tens by 4
$20 \times 4 = 80$

```
   t  o
   2  0
×     4
───────
   8  0
```

There are 80 oranges in the 4 boxes altogether.

Guided Practice

Multiply.

1 3 × 4 = ▢

3 × 40 = ▢

3 × 4 tens

2 4 × 8 = ▢

4 × 80 = ▢

4 × 8 tens

3 3 × 20 = ▢

3 × 40 = ▢

3 × 80 = ▢

What is 3 × 30?

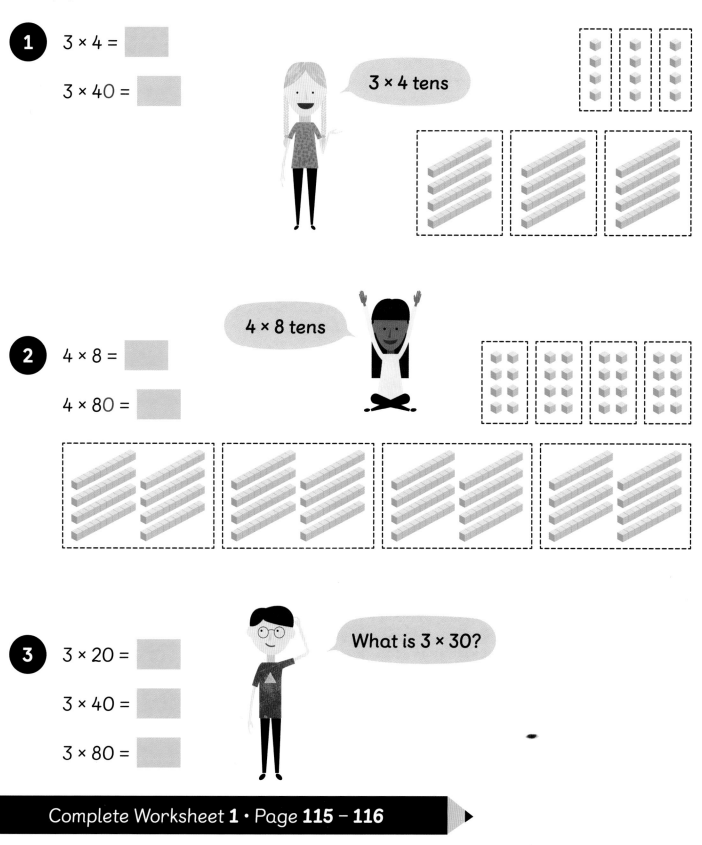

Complete Worksheet 1 · Page 115 – 116

Multiplying 2-Digit Numbers

In Focus

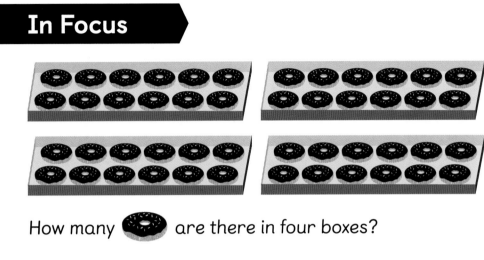

How many 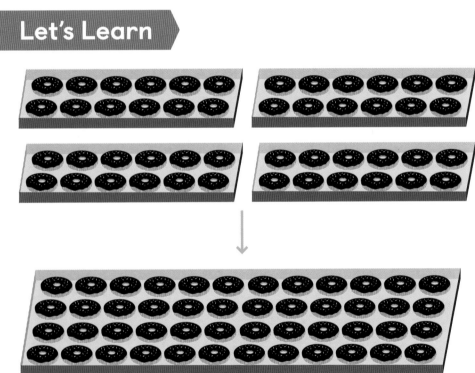 are there in four boxes?

Let's Learn

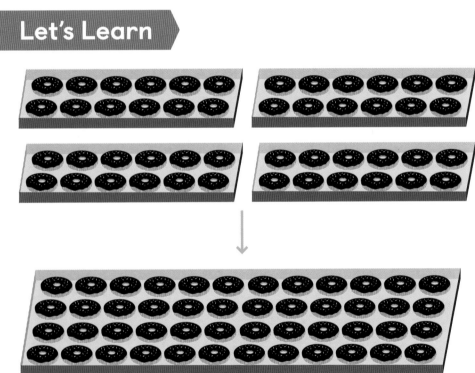

Method 1

12 + 12 + 12 + 12 = 48

There are 48 🍩 in four boxes.

Method 2

$12 \times 4 =$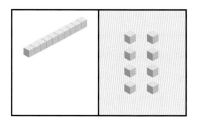

Multiply 12 by 4.

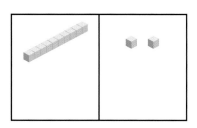

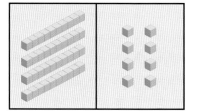

Step 1   Multiply the ones by 4.

2 ones × 4 = 8 ones

Step 2   Multiply the tens by 4.

1 ten × 4 = 4 tens

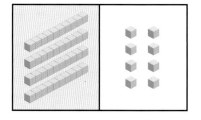

Step 3   2 ones × 4 = 8
1 ten × 4 = 40
12 × 4 = 8 + 40 = 48

There are 48 🍩 in four boxes.

12 × 4 = 48

⑩   ②

10 × 4   2 × 4

Guided Practice

Multiply.

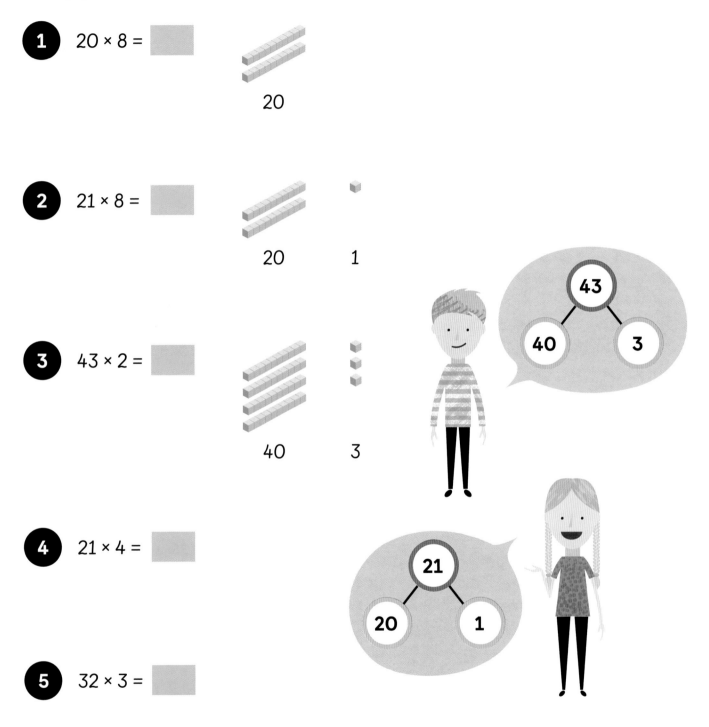

1 20 × 8 =

20

2 21 × 8 =

20   1

43
40   3

3 43 × 2 =

40   3

4 21 × 4 =

21
20   1

5 32 × 3 =

Complete Worksheet **2** · Page **117 – 118**

Multiplying 2-Digit Numbers

In Focus

There are 23 children in a class.
How many children are there in 2 classes?

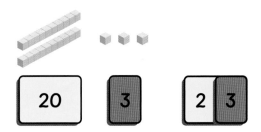

| | 20 | | 3 | | 2 | 3 |

Let's Learn

23

20   3

Step 1   Multiply the ones by 2.

3 ones × 2 = 6 ones

	t	o
	2	3
×		2
		6

Step 2   Multiply the tens by 2.

2 tens × 2 = 4 tens

	t	o
	2	3
×		2
		6
	4	0

Step 3   Add the products.

6 + 40 = 46

	t	o
	2	3
×		2
		6
+	4	0
	4	6

23 × 2 = 46

There are 46 children in the 2 classes.

Multiply.

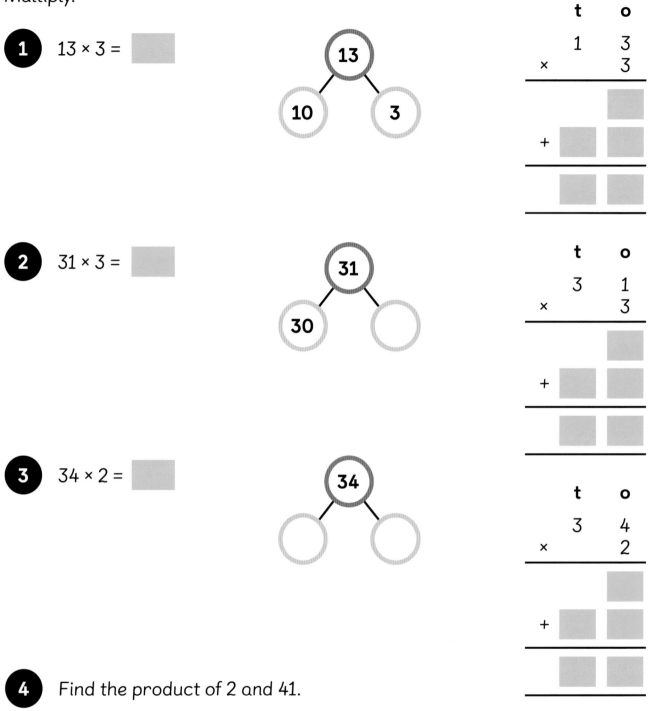

1 13 × 3 =

2 31 × 3 =

3 34 × 2 =

4 Find the product of 2 and 41.

Complete Worksheet **3** · Page **119**

Multiplying with Regrouping

In Focus

One tank has 23 fish.
How many fish are there in 4 tanks?

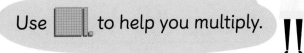
Use to help you multiply.

Let's Learn

1 There are 4 groups of 23 fish.
How do we multiply 23 by 4?

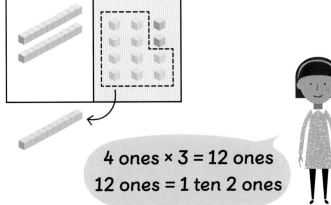

4 ones × 3 = 12 ones
12 ones = 1 ten 2 ones

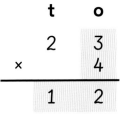

Step 1   Multiply the ones by 4.

	t	o
	2	3
×		4
	1	2

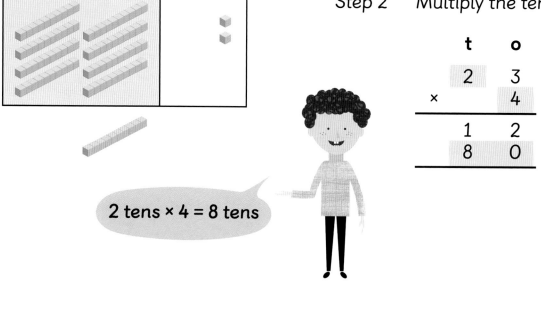

Step 2　Multiply the tens by 4.

	t	o
	2	3
×		4
	1	2
	8	0

2 tens × 4 = 8 tens

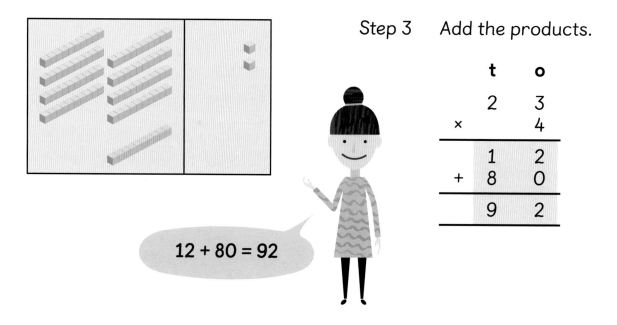

Step 3　Add the products.

	t	o
	2	3
×		4
	1	2
+	8	0
	9	2

12 + 80 = 92

23 × 4 = 92

There are 92 fish in 4 tanks.

2 Find the product of 25 and 4.

Method 1

This is 25.

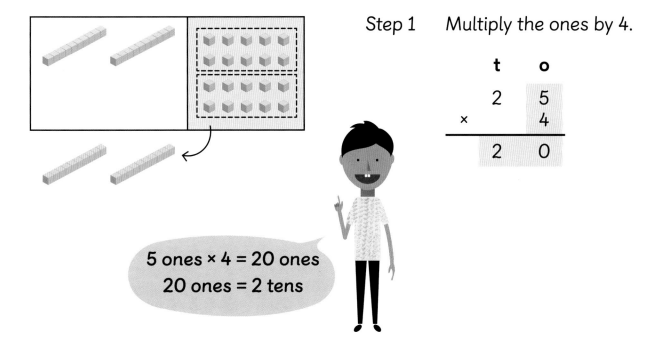

Step 1 Multiply the ones by 4.

```
      t   o
      2   5
  ×       4
  ─────────
      2   0
```

> 5 ones × 4 = 20 ones
> 20 ones = 2 tens

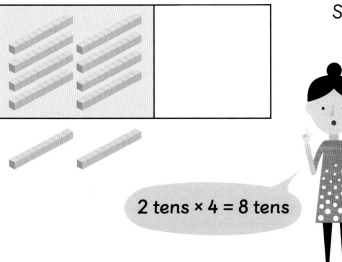

Step 2 Multiply the tens by 4.

```
      t   o
      2   5
  ×       4
  ─────────
      2   0
      8   0
```

> 2 tens × 4 = 8 tens

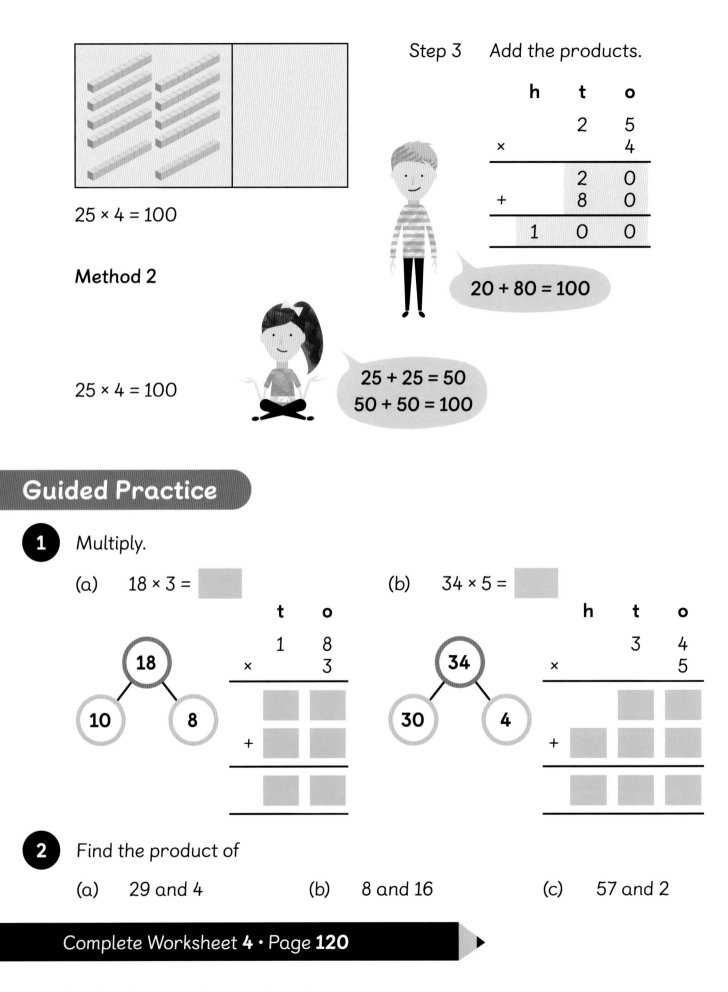

25 × 4 = 100

Method 2

25 × 4 = 100

25 + 25 = 50
50 + 50 = 100

Step 3   Add the products.

	h	t	o
		2	5
×			4
		2	0
+		8	0
	1	0	0

20 + 80 = 100

Guided Practice

1 Multiply.

(a)   18 × 3 =

	t	o
	1	8
×		3
+		

18
10   8

(b)   34 × 5 =

	h	t	o
		3	4
×			5
+			

34
30   4

2 Find the product of

(a)   29 and 4   (b)   8 and 16   (c)   57 and 2

Complete Worksheet 4 · Page 120

Multiplying with Regrouping

In Focus

This is how Hannah did 47 × 4.
Is she correct?

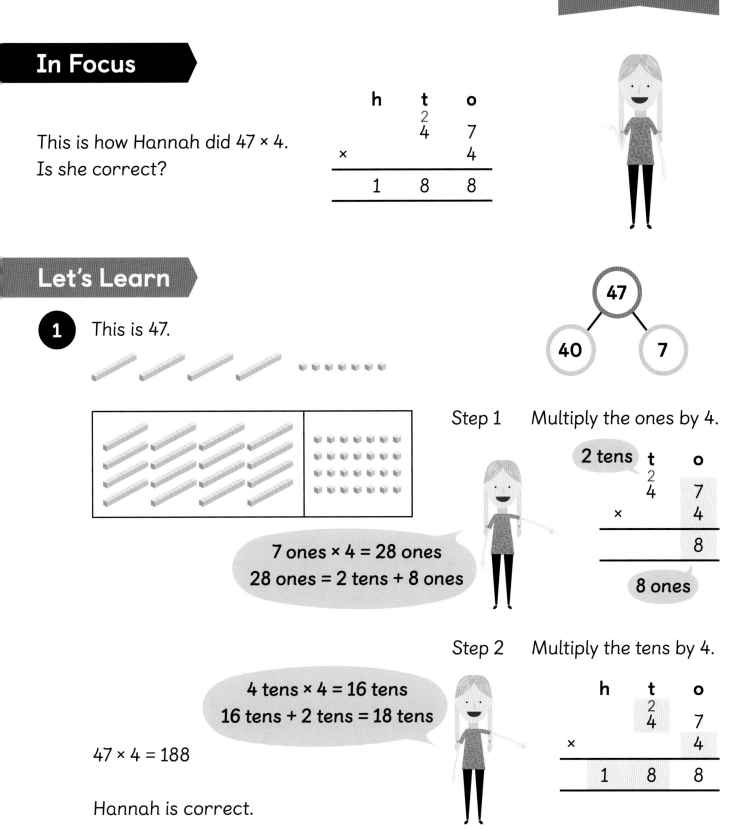

Let's Learn

1 This is 47.

Step 1 Multiply the ones by 4.

7 ones × 4 = 28 ones
28 ones = 2 tens + 8 ones

2 tens

8 ones

Step 2 Multiply the tens by 4.

4 tens × 4 = 16 tens
16 tens + 2 tens = 18 tens

47 × 4 = 188

Hannah is correct.

2 Use Hannah's method to find the product of 23 and 8.

Step 1

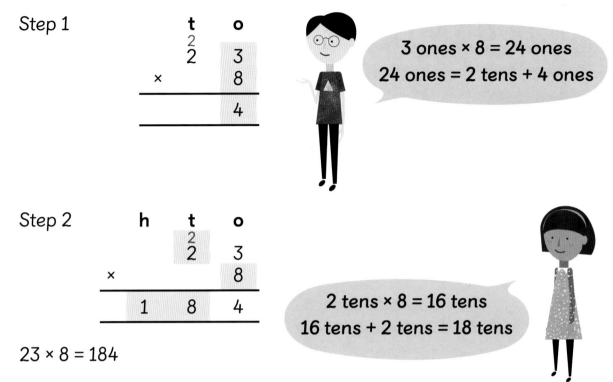

3 ones × 8 = 24 ones
24 ones = 2 tens + 4 ones

Step 2

2 tens × 8 = 16 tens
16 tens + 2 tens = 18 tens

23 × 8 = 184

The product of 23 and 8 is 184.

Guided Practice

Multiply.

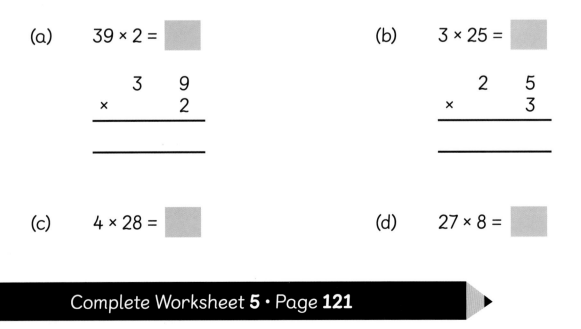

(a) 39 × 2 =

(b) 3 × 25 =

(c) 4 × 28 =

(d) 27 × 8 =

Complete Worksheet **5** · Page **121**

Simple Dividing

In Focus

Sam and Charles share 68 sweets equally among themselves.
How many sweets will each person get?

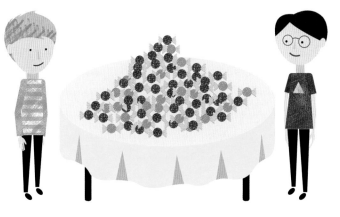

Let's Learn

To find the number of sweets each person gets, divide 68 by 2.

$68 \div 2 = $ ▢

Step 1   Divide 6 tens by 2.

6 tens ÷ 2
= 3 tens

6 tens ÷ 2

Step 2   Divide 8 ones by 2.

8 ones ÷ 2
= 4 ones

6 tens ÷ 2   8 ones ÷ 2

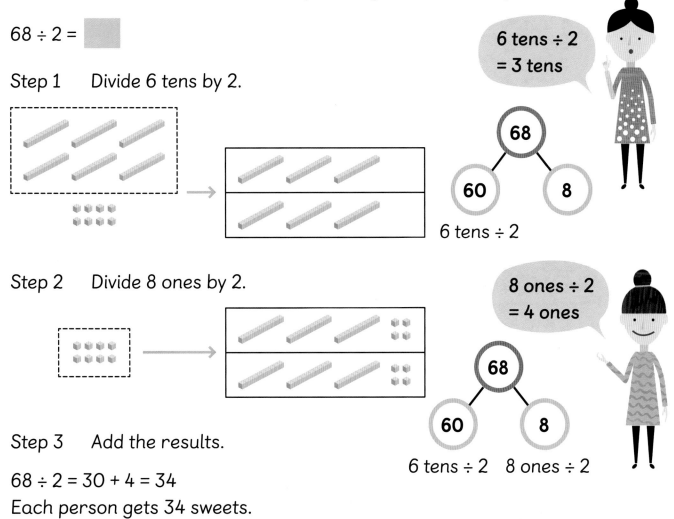

Step 3   Add the results.

$68 \div 2 = 30 + 4 = 34$
Each person gets 34 sweets.

Divide.

Use 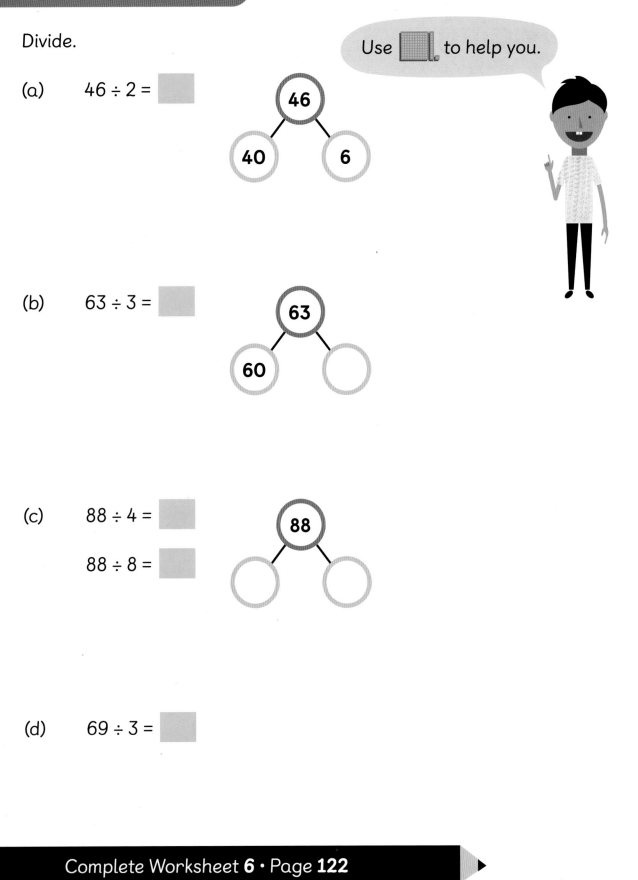 to help you.

(a) 46 ÷ 2 = ▢

(b) 63 ÷ 3 = ▢

(c) 88 ÷ 4 = ▢

   88 ÷ 8 = ▢

(d) 69 ÷ 3 = ▢

Complete Worksheet 6 · Page 122

Dividing with Regrouping

In Focus

A shopkeeper has 52 ice creams.
She packs them equally into 4 boxes.
How many ice creams are there in each box?

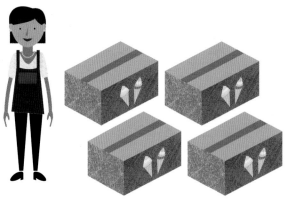

Let's Learn

To find the number of ice creams in each box, divide 52 by 4.

$52 \div 4 = $ ▢

Step 1   Split 52 into 40 and 12.

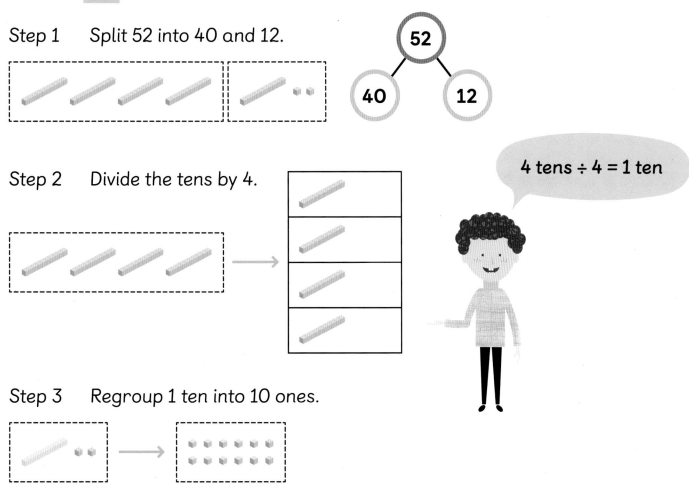

Step 2   Divide the tens by 4.

4 tens ÷ 4 = 1 ten

Step 3   Regroup 1 ten into 10 ones.

Step 4 Divide the ones by 4.

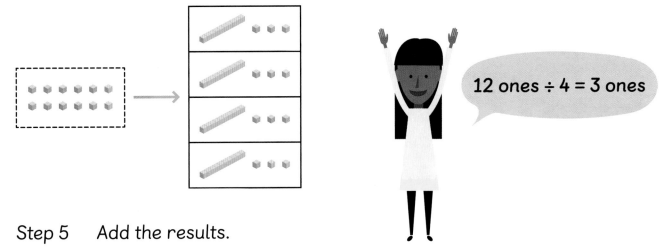

12 ones ÷ 4 = 3 ones

Step 5 Add the results.

52 ÷ 4 = 10 + 3 = 13

There are 13 ice creams in each box.

Guided Practice

Use 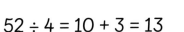 to help you.

Divide.

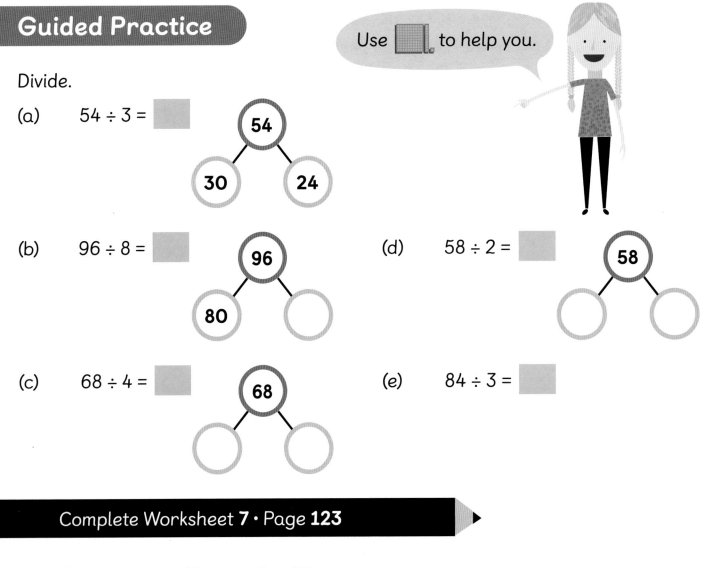

(a) 54 ÷ 3 = ☐

54
30   24

(b) 96 ÷ 8 = ☐

96
80   ◯

(c) 68 ÷ 4 = ☐

68
◯   ◯

(d) 58 ÷ 2 = ☐

58
◯   ◯

(e) 84 ÷ 3 = ☐

Complete Worksheet 7 · Page 123

Dividing with Regrouping

In Focus

Charles learns this way to divide 96 ÷ 8.

96 ÷ 8 = 12

What is Charles doing?

```
      1   2
8 ⟌  9   6
   -  8   0
      1   6
   -  1   6
          0
```

Let's Learn

96

80   16

First, I take 80 from 96.
Then, I take 16 from
the remaining 16.

```
      1   2
8 ⟌  9   6
   -  8   0
      1   6
   -  1   6
          0
```

96

80   16

1 ten

```
      1   2
8 ⟌  9   6
   -  8   0
      1   6
   -  1   6
          0
```

8 tens ÷ 8 = 1 ten

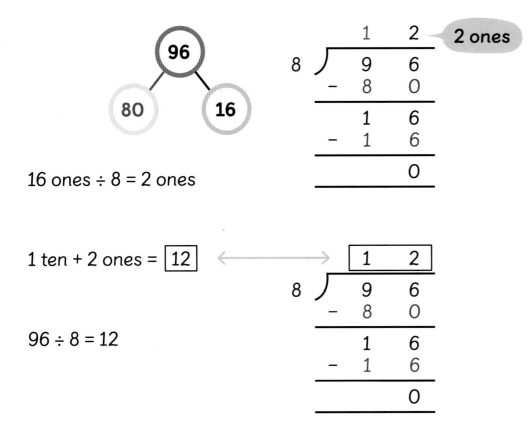

16 ones ÷ 8 = 2 ones

1 ten + 2 ones = 12 ⟵⟶

96 ÷ 8 = 12

Guided Practice

Use Charles' method to divide.

(a) 92 ÷ 2 =

(b) 72 ÷ 3 =

(c) 56 ÷ 4 =

(d) 75 ÷ 5 =

(e) 96 ÷ 4 =

Complete Worksheet **8** • Page **124**

Solving Word Problems

In Focus

There are 18 blue crayons on the table.
There are twice as many green crayons
as blue crayons on another table.

(a)   How many green crayons are there?

(b)   How many crayons are there altogether?

Let's Learn

1   (a)

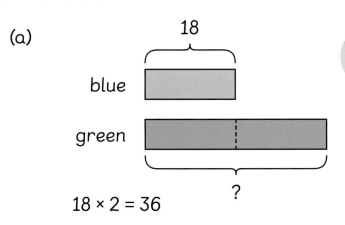

18 × 2 = 36

There are 36 green crayons.

'Twice' means
2 times.

(b)

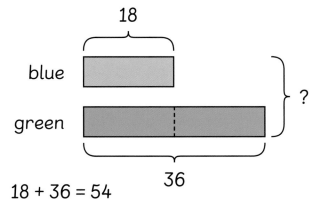

18 + 36 = 54

There are 54 crayons altogether.

2 There are 28 boys in a group.

There are 3 times as many girls as there are boys.

(a)   How many girls are there?

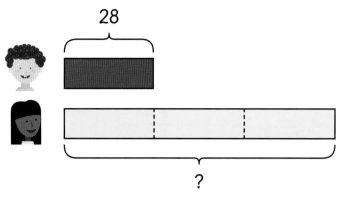

28 × 3 = 84

There are 84 girls.

(b)   How many children are there?

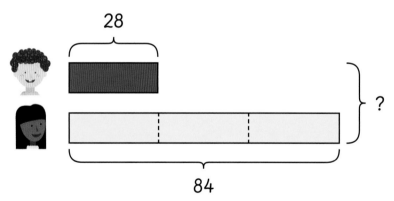

28 + 84 = 112

There are 112 children altogether.

Solve.

1 Ravi has 29 coins.
Holly has 3 times as many coins as Ravi has.
(a) How many coins does Holly have?
(b) How many coins are there altogether?

2 There are 24 boxes with the same number of berries inside.
Each box contains 4 strawberries and 4 blueberries.
How many berries are there altogether?

3 Ruby has 32 sheets of paper.
She cuts 4 square pieces and 3 triangle pieces
from each sheet of paper.
How many pieces does she cut in all?

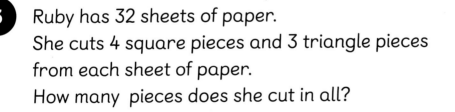

Complete Worksheet **9** • Page **125 – 126**

Solving Word Problems

In Focus

I have 36 beads.

She has twice as many beads as I have.

How many beads do the children have altogether?

Emma   Sam

Let's Learn

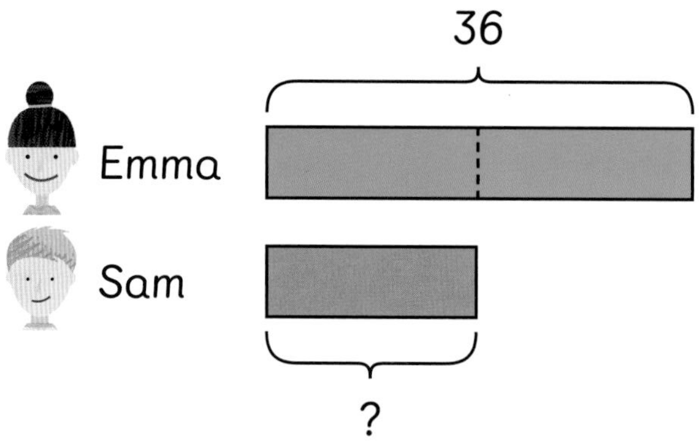

Emma

Sam

36

?

$36 \div 2 = 18$

Sam has 18 beads.

Emma

Sam

36

?

18

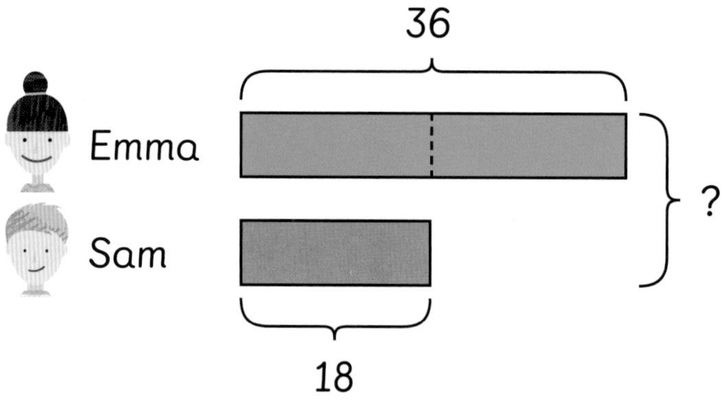

$36 + 18 = 54$

The children have 54 beads altogether.

Solve.

1 There are three times as many boys as there are girls in a hall.
There are 78 boys in the hall.
(a) How many girls are there in the hall?
(b) How many children are there in the hall?

2 There are four times as many children
as there are adults at the Science Museum.
The number of boys is equal to the number of girls.
Altogether, there are 80 visitors at the Science Museum.
How many boys are there at the Science Museum?

3 Holly makes 2 cups of tea a day.
She uses 3 sugar cubes for every cup of tea.
A jar contains 48 sugar cubes.
(a) How many cups of tea can Holly make from
a jar of sugar cubes?
(b) How many days does she take to use up
the entire jar of sugar cubes?

Complete Worksheet 10 · Page 127 – 128

Solving Word Problems

In Focus

Sam, Ravi and Elliott have 92 marbles altogether.
Sam has 3 times as many marbles as Ravi.
Ravi has 2 fewer marbles than Elliott.
How many marbles does Ravi have?

Let's Learn

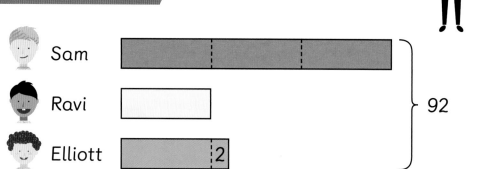

Sam

Ravi

Elliott ⟨2

⎫
⎬ 92
⎭

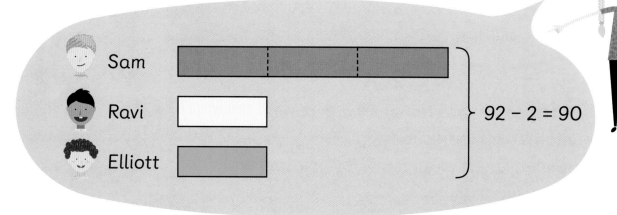

Sam

Ravi

Elliott

⎫
⎬ 92 − 2 = 90
⎭

[   ] = 90 ÷ 5
= 18

90
50   40

Ravi has 18 marbles.

Solve.

1 There are 12 more girls than boys in the football club.
There are 94 children in the club.
How many girls are there in the club?

2 Lulu, Hannah and Ruby have 26 dolls altogether.
Lulu has 5 times as many dolls as Hannah.
Hannah has 2 more dolls than Ruby.
How many dolls does Hannah have?

Complete Worksheet **11** · Page **129**

Mind Workout

Tickets for a school concert were sold to adults and children at different prices as shown in the table.

	price per ticket
adult	£6
child	£3

On the first day of sales, the same number of adult tickets and child tickets were sold.

The total amount of money collected from the sale of tickets was £72.

How many adult tickets were sold that day?

Complete the word problem.
Ask your classmates to solve the problem.

|_____| has |_____| |_____|.
(name)　　　　　　(2-digit number)　　(objects)

|_____| has |___| times as many |_____| as |_____|.
(name)　　　　　　(1-digit number)　　　　　　　(objects)　　　　　(name)

How many |_____| do |_____| and |_____|
(objects)　　　　　　(name)　　　　　　　(name)

have altogether?

I know how to...

☐ multiply a 2-digit number by a 1-digit number.

☐ multiply without regrouping.

☐ multiply with regrouping.

☐ divide a 2-digit number by a 1-digit number.

☐ divide without regrouping.

☐ divide with regrouping.

☐ solve word problems on multiplication.

☐ solve word problems on division.

Self Check

How tall is Ravi?

How long is the table?

Chapter 5
Length

Writing Length in Metres and Centimetres

In Focus

The length of the table is more than 1 metre.
What is the length of the table?

Let's Learn

1 We use a tape measure to measure lengths longer than 1 metre.

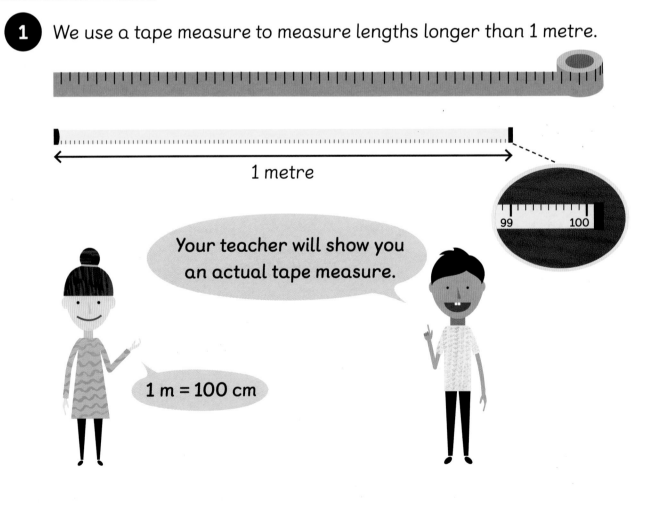

1 metre

99   100

Your teacher will show you an actual tape measure.

1 m = 100 cm

2 What is the length of the table?

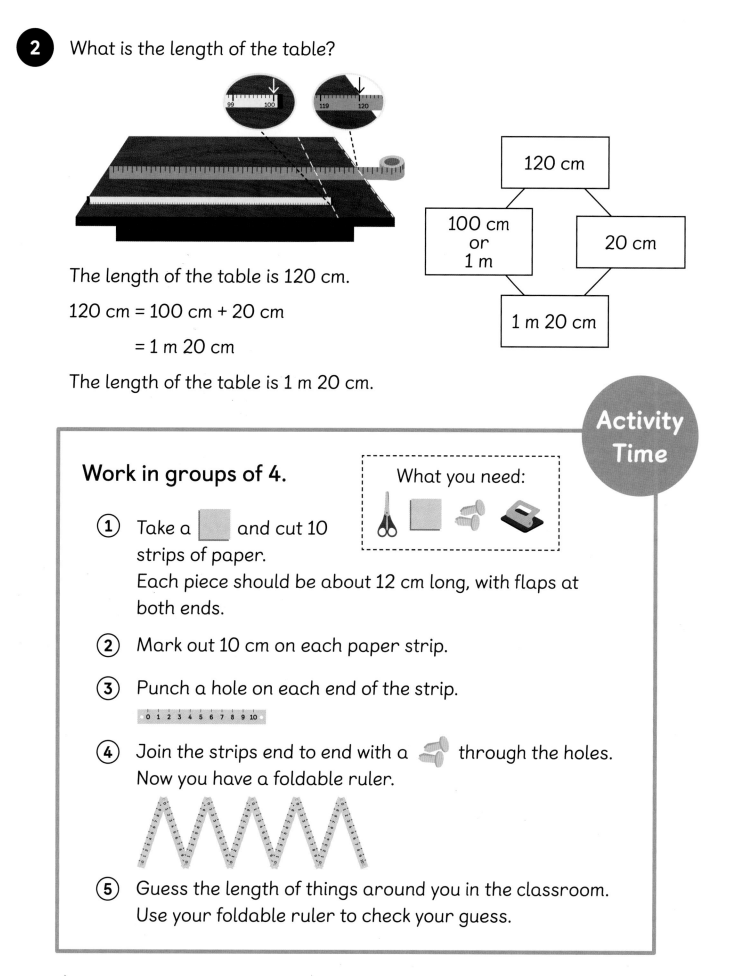

The length of the table is 120 cm.

120 cm = 100 cm + 20 cm

    = 1 m 20 cm

The length of the table is 1 m 20 cm.

| 120 cm |
| 100 cm or 1 m |
| 20 cm |
| 1 m 20 cm |

Activity Time

Work in groups of 4.

What you need:

① Take a ▢ and cut 10 strips of paper.
Each piece should be about 12 cm long, with flaps at both ends.

② Mark out 10 cm on each paper strip.

③ Punch a hole on each end of the strip.

`0 1 2 3 4 5 6 7 8 9 10`

④ Join the strips end to end with a 🔩 through the holes.
Now you have a foldable ruler.

⑤ Guess the length of things around you in the classroom.
Use your foldable ruler to check your guess.

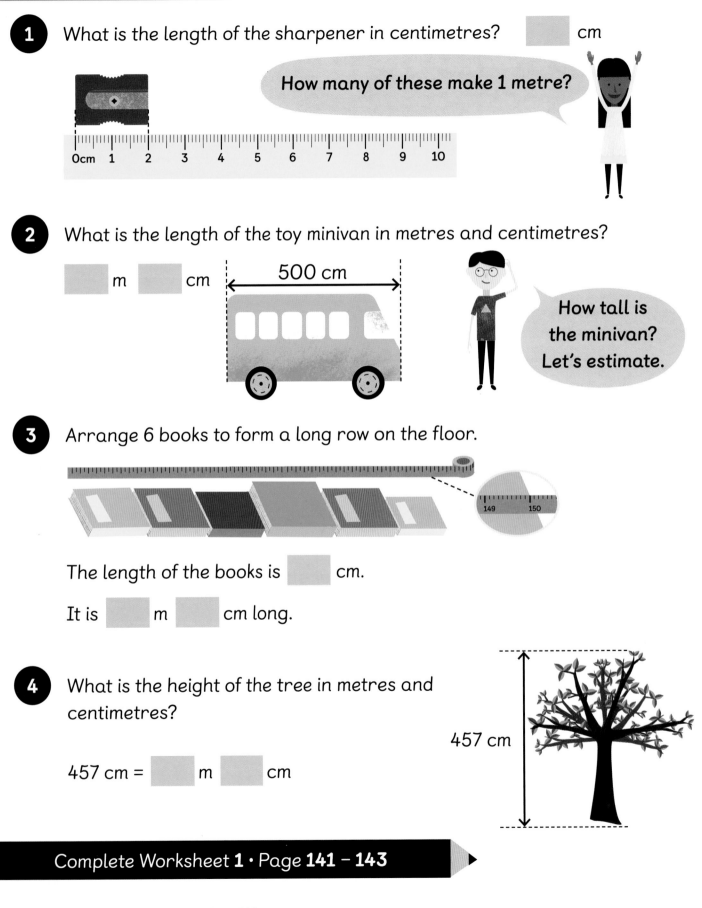

1 What is the length of the sharpener in centimetres? [ ] cm

How many of these make 1 metre?

0cm 1 2 3 4 5 6 7 8 9 10

2 What is the length of the toy minivan in metres and centimetres?

[ ] m [ ] cm

500 cm

How tall is the minivan? Let's estimate.

3 Arrange 6 books to form a long row on the floor.

149   150

The length of the books is [ ] cm.

It is [ ] m [ ] cm long.

4 What is the height of the tree in metres and centimetres?

457 cm = [ ] m [ ] cm

457 cm

Complete Worksheet 1 · Page 141 – 143

Writing Length in Centimetres

In Focus

What is Ravi's height in centimetres?

Let's Learn

1 We use a tape measure to measure Ravi's height.

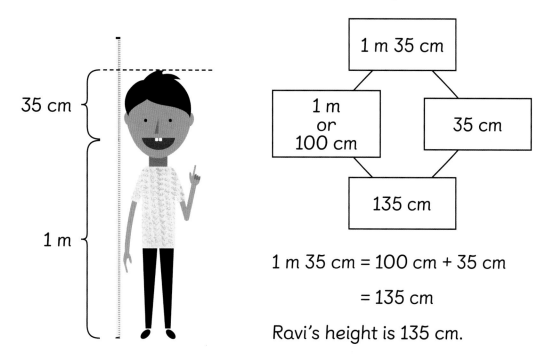

35 cm

1 m

1 m 35 cm

1 m
or
100 cm

35 cm

135 cm

1 m 35 cm = 100 cm + 35 cm

= 135 cm

Ravi's height is 135 cm.

How tall is each person in centimetres?

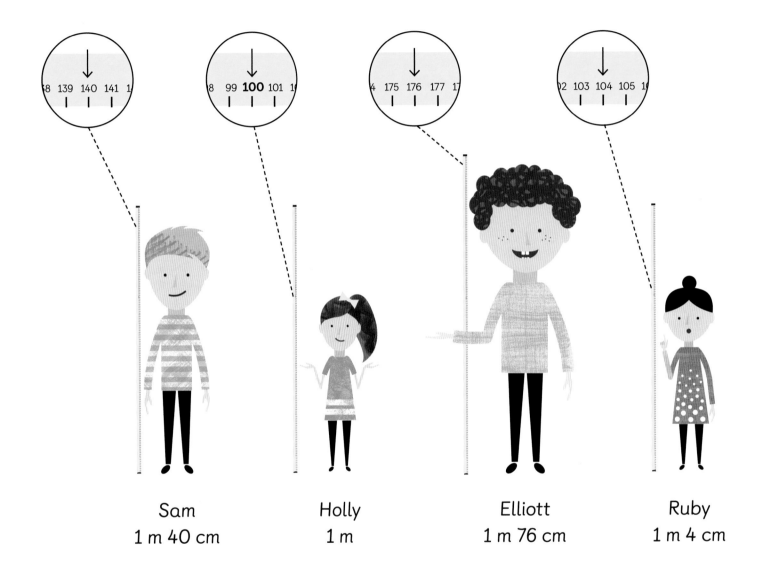

Sam	Holly	Elliott	Ruby
1 m 40 cm	1 m	1 m 76 cm	1 m 4 cm

Complete Worksheet 2 • Page **144 – 145**

Writing Length in Metres

In Focus

Distance is used to describe the length between one place and another.

What is the distance between the zoo and the bird park?

Let's Learn

1

19 km

The distance between the zoo and the bird park is about 19 **kilometres**. We write km for kilometre.

1 kilometre is the same as 1000 metres.

1 km = 1000 m

Kilometre, or km, is another unit of length. We use km for long distances.

2 The length of the football pitch is 100 m.

100 m

The length of 10 football pitches is about 1000 m or 1 km.

1 km

Do you know a place that is about 1 km away from your school? How can you tell the distance from your school to that place?

3

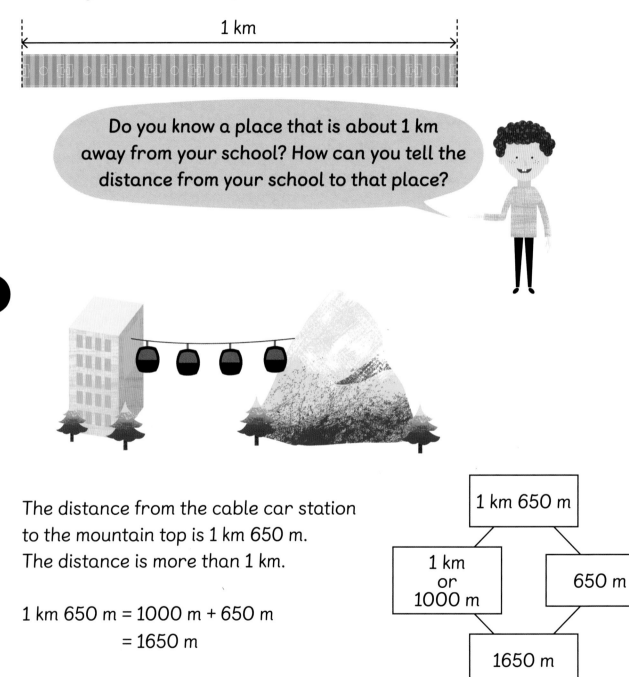

The distance from the cable car station to the mountain top is 1 km 650 m. The distance is more than 1 km.

1 km 650 m = 1000 m + 650 m
　　　　　　 = 1650 m

1 km 650 m

1 km or 1000 m

650 m

1650 m

1 Write in metres.

(a)   1 km 400 m = _____ m

(b)   3 km 45 m = _____ m

(c)   5 km 5 m = _____ m

2 Look at the map and answer the questions.

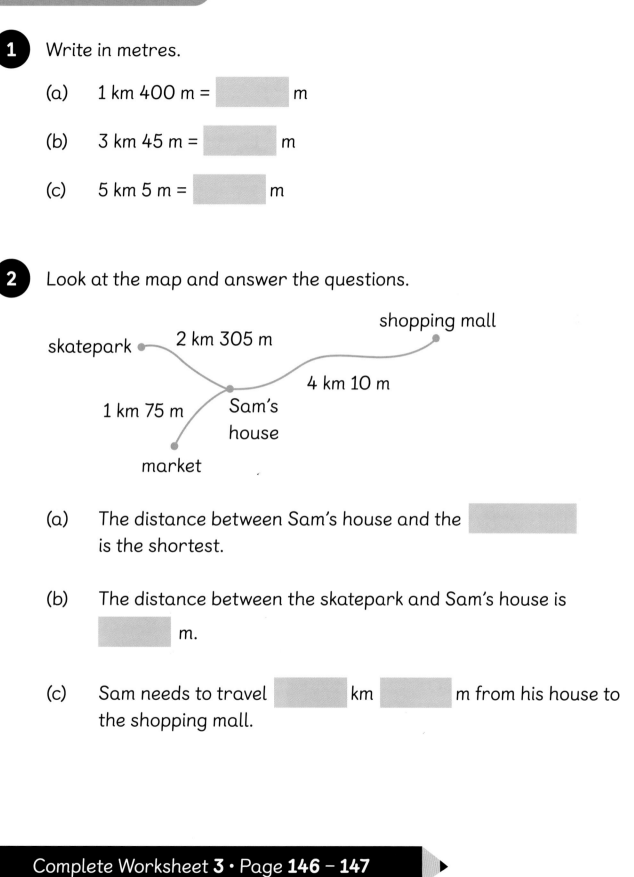

(a)   The distance between Sam's house and the _____ is the shortest.

(b)   The distance between the skatepark and Sam's house is _____ m.

(c)   Sam needs to travel _____ km _____ m from his house to the shopping mall.

Complete Worksheet 3 · Page 146 – 147 ▶

Writing Length in Kilometres and Metres

In Focus

Ravi won a race.
He ran 1500 m.
What was the distance Ravi ran
in kilometres and metres?

Let's Learn

```
        ┌─────────────┐
        │   1500 m    │
        └─────────────┘
        ╱             ╲
┌──────────┐      ┌──────────┐
│ 1000 m   │      │  500 m   │
│   or     │      └──────────┘
│  1 km    │
└──────────┘
        ╲             ╱
        ┌─────────────┐
        │ 1 km 500 m  │
        └─────────────┘
```

1 km = 1000 m

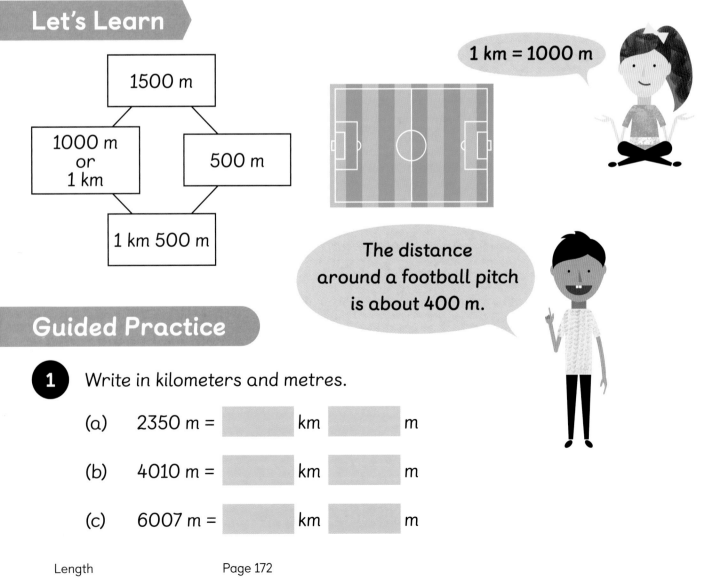

The distance
around a football pitch
is about 400 m.

Guided Practice

1. Write in kilometers and metres.

   (a) 2350 m = [ ] km [ ] m

   (b) 4010 m = [ ] km [ ] m

   (c) 6007 m = [ ] km [ ] m

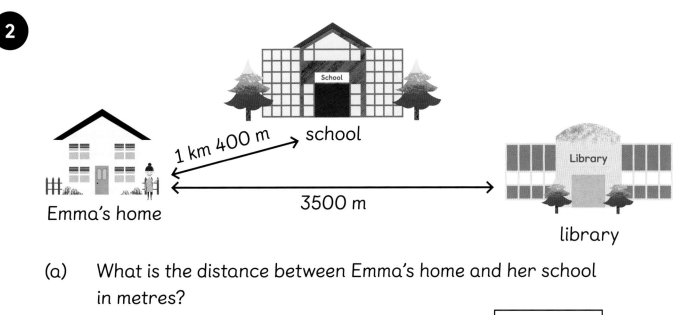

2

Emma's home — 1 km 400 m → school

3500 m → library

(a) What is the distance between Emma's home and her school in metres?

1 km 400 m = ⬜ m + ⬜ m

= ⬜ m

The distance between Emma's home and her school is ⬜ m.

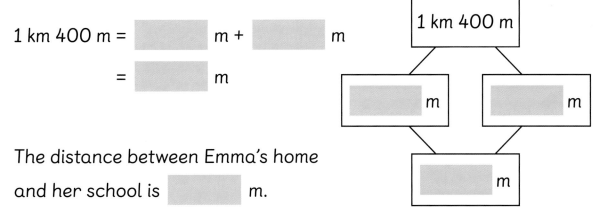

1 km 400 m

⬜ m   ⬜ m

⬜ m

(b) What is the distance between Emma's home and the library in kilometres and metres?

3500 m = ⬜ m + ⬜ m

= ⬜ km ⬜ m

The distance between Emma's home and the library is ⬜ km ⬜ m.

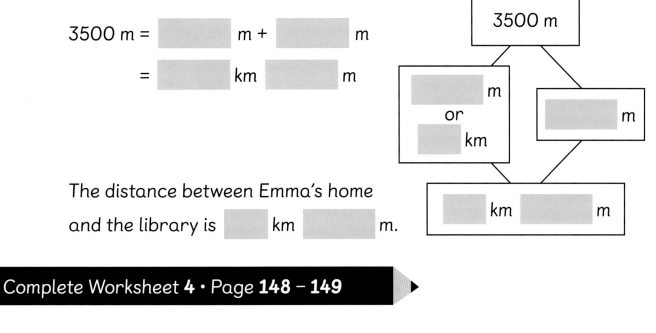

3500 m

⬜ m
or
⬜ km

⬜ m

⬜ km ⬜ m

Complete Worksheet **4** · Page **148 – 149**

Comparing Length

In Focus

name	height
Hannah	155 cm
Charles	1 m 50 cm
Lulu	105 cm
Elliott	1 m 60 cm
Holly	98 cm

Who is taller? Charles or Lulu?

Let's Learn

Charles

Lulu

1 m 50 cm

105 cm

Method 1

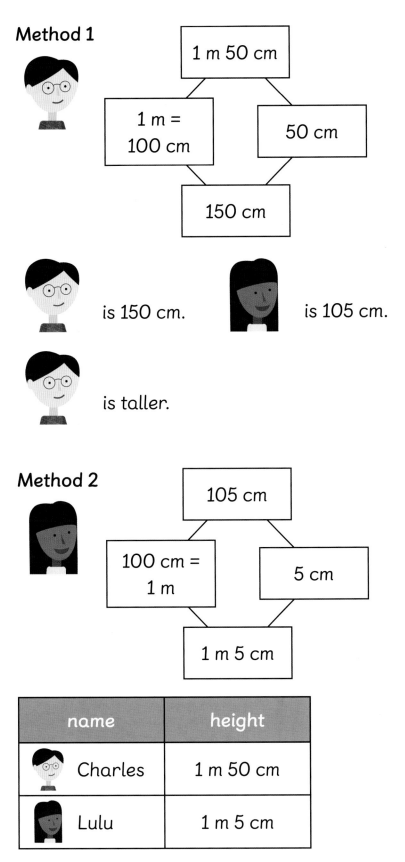

1 m 50 cm

1 m = 100 cm

50 cm

150 cm

is 150 cm.

is 105 cm.

is taller.

Method 2

105 cm

100 cm = 1 m

5 cm

1 m 5 cm

name	height
Charles	1 m 50 cm
Lulu	1 m 5 cm

is taller.

1

I ran 2 km 45 m.

Ruby

I ran 2450 m.

Amira

Who ran a longer distance?

2 Sam ran 5 km 80 m last week.
This week he ran 5800 m.
Next week, he plans to run 580 m.

Which distance is longer?

580 m or 5800 m?

5 km 80 m or 5800 m?

Complete Worksheet 5 • Page 150 – 151

Solving Word Problems

In Focus

Ravi used a wooden board with the length of 315 cm to make a bookshelf.
He used another wooden board with the length of 235 cm to make a shoe rack.
What was the total length of the wooden boards used?

Let's Learn

1

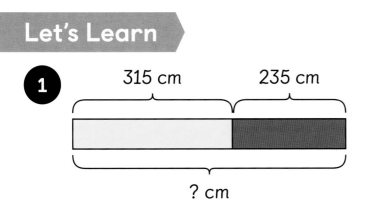

315 cm   235 cm

? cm

315 + 235 = 550

The total length of wooden boards used was 550 cm.

2 Charles used 315 cm from a piece of wooden board that was 500 cm long. How long was the piece left over?

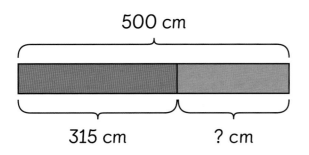

500 cm

315 cm   ? cm

500 − 315 = 185

The piece left over was 185 cm long.

Guided Practice

1

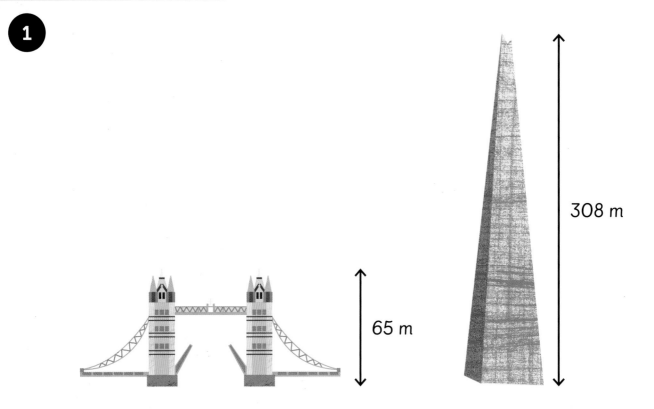

65 m

308 m

How much taller is the Shard than Tower Bridge?

2

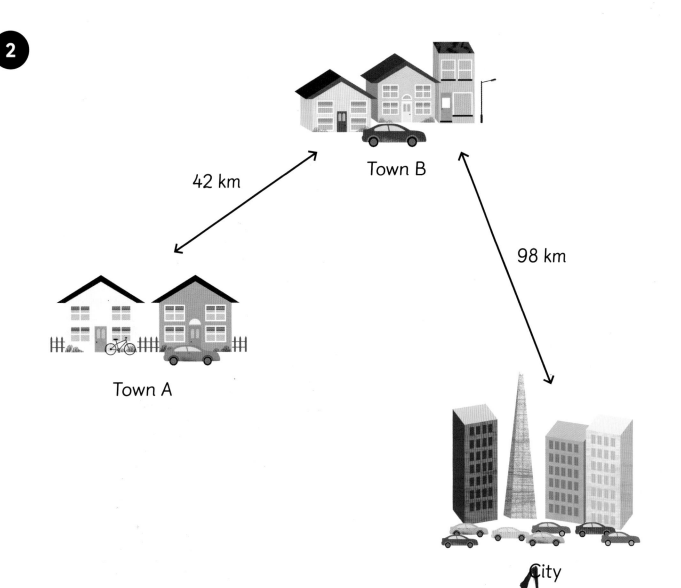

42 km

Town B

98 km

Town A

City

Emma travels from Town A to the City, passing through Town B.
Find the total distance she travels.

Complete Worksheet **6** · Page **152 – 153**

Solving Word Problems

In Focus

Hannah had 5 m of yarn.
She used 74 cm of it.

How much yarn did Hannah have left?

Let's Learn

Method 1

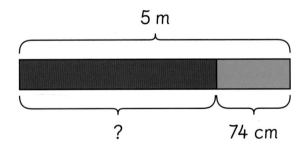

5 m

?   74 cm

500 − 74 = 426

She had 426 cm of yarn left.

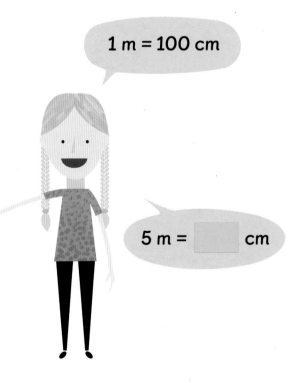

1 m = 100 cm

5 m = ⬜ cm

Method 2

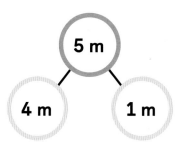

1 m = 100 cm

100 − 74 = 26

She had 4 m 26 cm of yarn left.

Guided Practice

1 A piece of red ribbon is 1 m long.
A piece of blue ribbon is 89 cm long.
Find their total length in centimeters.

2 Elliott had a 3 m rope.
He used some and had 64 cm of it left.
How much rope did he use?

3

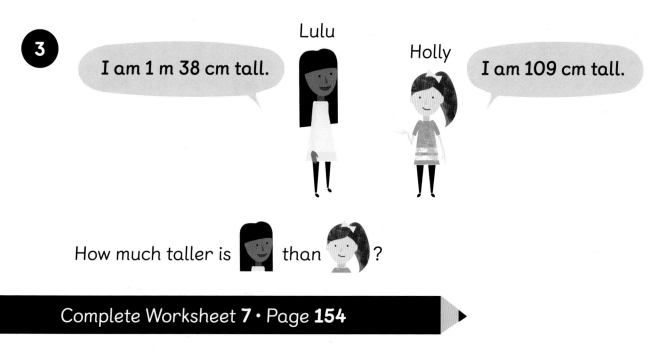

I am 1 m 38 cm tall.

Lulu

Holly

I am 109 cm tall.

How much taller is [ ] than [ ] ?

Complete Worksheet 7 • Page 154

Solving Word Problems

In Focus

A tailor needs 3 m of cloth to make a shirt.
He made 47 shirts and had 7 m of cloth left over.

How much cloth did the tailor have at first?

Let's Learn

How much cloth did he use to make the shirts?

$50 \times 3 = 150$

$47 \times 3 = 150 -$ ☐

```
      4  7
   ×     3
   -------
      2  1
 + 1  2  0
   -------
   1  4  1
```

1 shirt

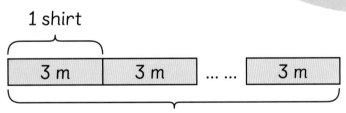

47 shirts

$47 \times 3 = 141$

He used 141 m of the cloth.

$141 + 7 = 148$

How much cloth did the tailor have at first?

He had 148 m of cloth at first.

Guided Practice

1 Ruby needs 2 m of cloth to make a shirt.
How much cloth does she need to make 23 shirts?

2 A school banner is 5 times as long as a classroom poster.
The classroom poster is 98 cm long.
What is the length of the school banner?
Give your answer in metres and centimetres.

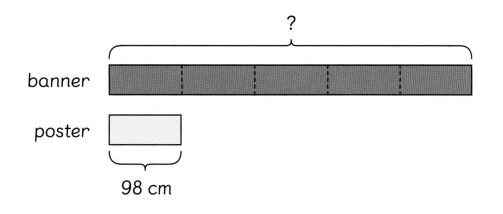

banner

poster

98 cm

3 Amira's ribbon is 75 cm long.
Emma's ribbon is 3 times as long as Amira's ribbon.
What is the total length of their ribbons?

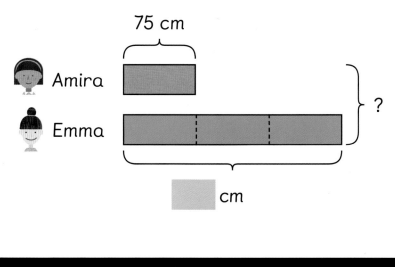

75 cm

Amira

Emma

?

cm

Complete Worksheet 8 · Page 155 – 156

Solving Word Problems

In Focus

Garden City is 3 times as far from Happy Town as it is from Red Town.
Garden City is 72 km from Happy Town.

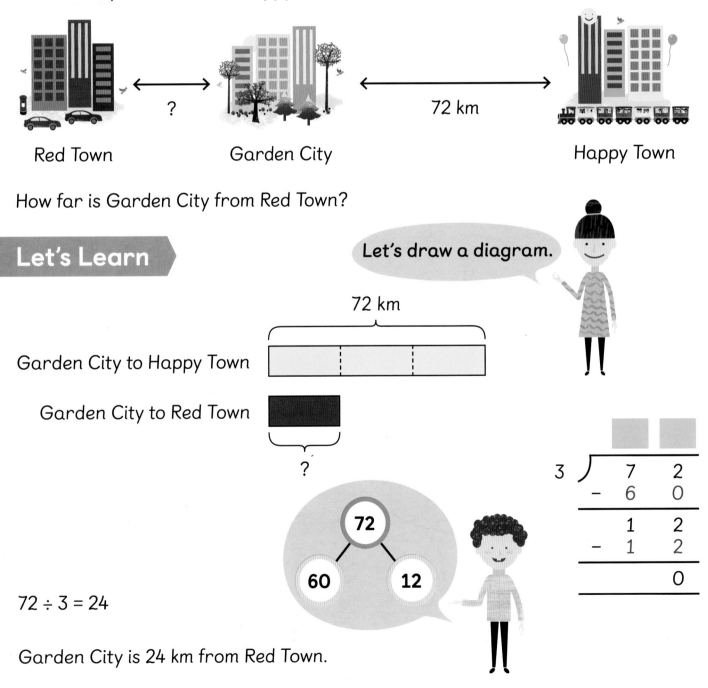

How far is Garden City from Red Town?

Let's Learn

Let's draw a diagram.

72 km

Garden City to Happy Town

Garden City to Red Town

?

72

60   12

$72 \div 3 = 24$

Garden City is 24 km from Red Town.

The blue ribbon is twice as long as the red one.
The blue ribbon is 3 times as long as the green one.
The green ribbon is 28 cm long.

(a)   Find the length of the blue ribbon.

(b)   Find the length of the red ribbon.

Complete Worksheet 9 · Page 157 – 158

Solving Word Problems

In Focus

Sam had 100 cm of cloth to make some mini flags.
Each flag uses the same length of cloth.
After making 3 flags, he had 19 cm of cloth left.

What is the length of cloth used to make each flag?

Let's Learn

100 cm

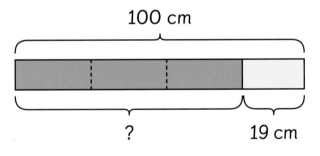

?   19 cm

$100 - 19 = 81$

81 cm

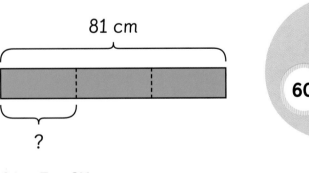

?

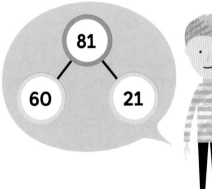

81
60   21

3) 8 1
  − 6 0
    2 1
  − 2 1
      0

$81 ÷ 3 = 27$

The length of cloth used to make each flag is 27 cm.

1 Ravi cut a 92 cm pole into 4 pieces of equal length.
Find the length of each piece.

2 Hannah wants to cut a 70 cm pole into 8 cm pieces.
What are the most pieces she can get?
How long is the leftover piece?

3 Charles had 250 cm of ribbon.
He cut the ribbon into 8 pieces of equal length and had some ribbon left.
Each piece of ribbon was 27 cm long.
How much ribbon was left over?

Complete Worksheet **10** • Page **159 – 160** ▶

Mind Workout ▶

5 girls stand in a straight row.
Each girl is 90 cm apart from the other.
Find the distance between the first and the last girl.

Act it out or draw a diagram to help you.

Write a word problem using this model.

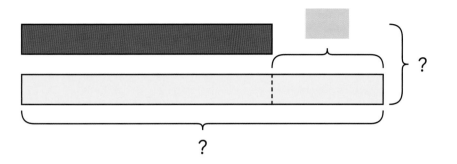

You may use the following to help you.

length	longer than	shorter than	total
cm	120	50	

I know how to...

☐ write length in metres (m) and centimetres (cm).

☐ convert length from m and cm to cm.

☐ convert length from cm to m and cm.

☐ write length in kilometers (km) and metres (m).

☐ convert length from km and m to m.

☐ convert length from m to km and m.

☐ compare different lengths.

☐ solve word problems on length.

Self Check

Chapter 6
Mass

Reading Weighing Scales

In Focus

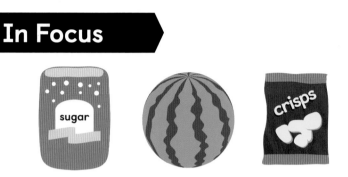

How can we find out which is the heaviest and which is the lightest?

Let's Learn

We use weighing scales.

The packet of crisps weighs about 200 g.

The watermelon weighs about 1 kg.

The bag of sugar weighs about 3 kg.

We say the mass of the bag of sugar is about 3 kg.

Which is the lightest?

Which is the heaviest?

How heavy is each thing?

(a)

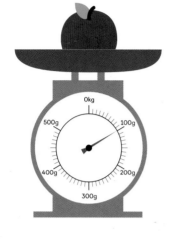

The apple weighs about ▢ g.

(b)

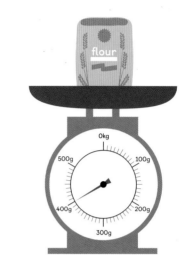

The packet of flour weighs about ▢ g.

(c)

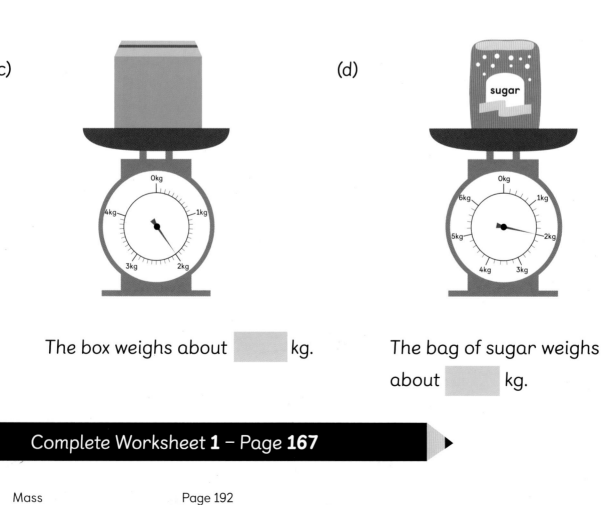

The box weighs about ▢ kg.

(d)

The bag of sugar weighs about ▢ kg.

Complete Worksheet **1** – Page **167**

Reading Weighing Scales

In Focus

The bag of crisps weighs more than 300 g.
It weighs less than 400 g.

What is the mass of the bag of crisps?

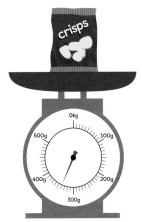

Let's Learn

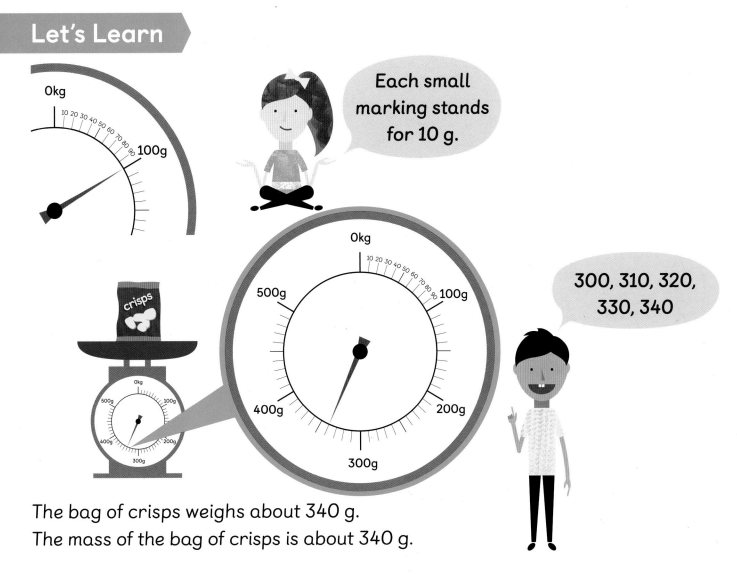

Each small marking stands for 10 g.

300, 310, 320, 330, 340

The bag of crisps weighs about 340 g.
The mass of the bag of crisps is about 340 g.

Guided Practice

How heavy is each thing?
Find its mass.

(a)

The mass of the bag of crisps
is about [   ] g.

(b)

The mass of the bowl is about
[   ] g.

(c)

The mass of the bag of crisps
and a mushroom is about
[   ] g.

Which is the lightest? [   ]

Which is the heaviest? [   ]

(d)

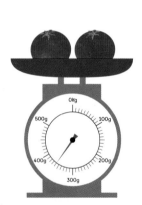

The mass of 2 tomatoes is about
[   ] g.

Complete Worksheet 2 – Page 168

Reading Weighing Scales

In Focus

The mass of is about 1 kg 200 g.

weighs about 1 kg 20 g.

Who is correct?

Let's Learn

Each small marking stands for 100 g.

100g

100g 100g

100g 100g 100g

100g 100g 100g 100g

1 kg = 1000 g

0kg

100 200 300 400 500 600 700 800 900

1kg

0kg

4kg 1kg

3kg 2kg

0kg

1kg

100 200

The watermelon weighs about 1 kg 200 g.
The mass of the watermelon is about 1 kg 200 g.

What is the mass of each thing?

(a)

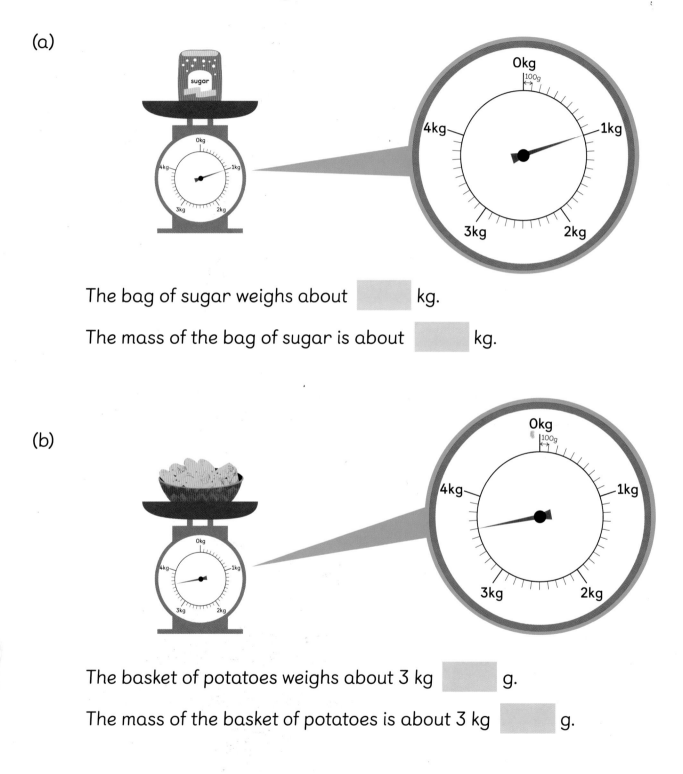

The bag of sugar weighs about ▢ kg.

The mass of the bag of sugar is about ▢ kg.

(b)

The basket of potatoes weighs about 3 kg ▢ g.

The mass of the basket of potatoes is about 3 kg ▢ g.

(c)

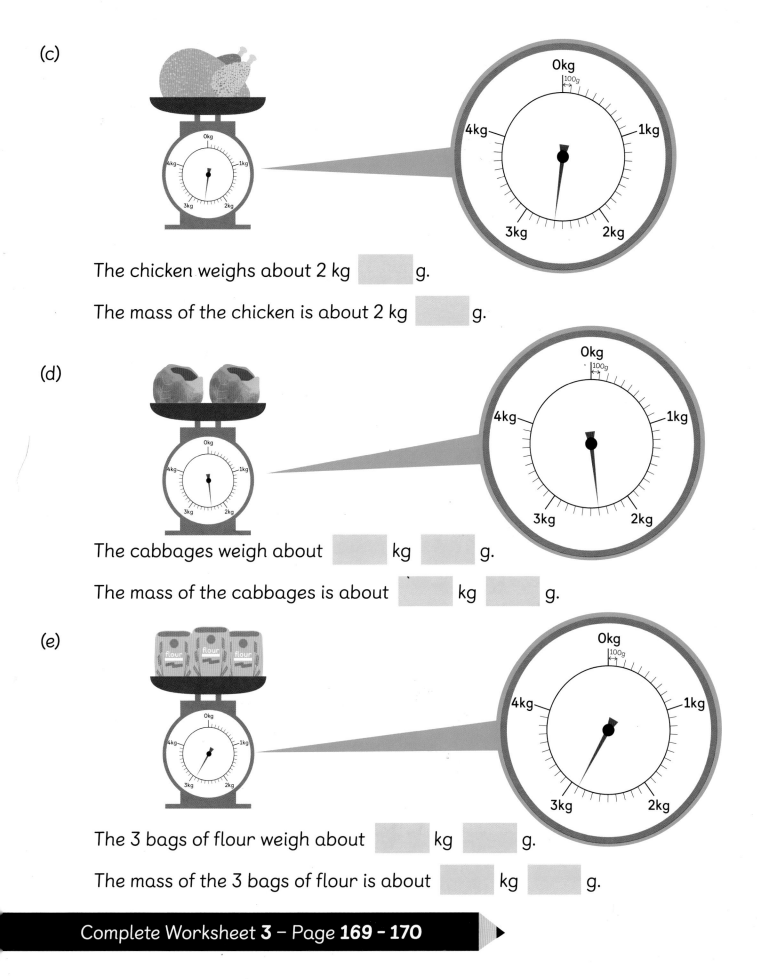

The chicken weighs about 2 kg [   ] g.

The mass of the chicken is about 2 kg [   ] g.

(d)

The cabbages weigh about [   ] kg [   ] g.

The mass of the cabbages is about [   ] kg [   ] g.

(e)

The 3 bags of flour weigh about [   ] kg [   ] g.

The mass of the 3 bags of flour is about [   ] kg [   ] g.

Complete Worksheet **3** – Page **169 – 170**

Reading Weighing Scales

In Focus

The mass of the bag of rice is more than 3 kg.
How can you tell its mass?

Let's Learn

Each small marking stands for 200 g.

The mass of the jar of jelly beans is about 1 kg 200 g.

The mass of the box is about 2 kg 400 g.

The mass of the bag of rice is about 3 kg 200 g.

Work in groups of 4.

What you need:

① Look at the things in your classroom.
Estimate the mass of each thing.

② Measure the actual mass of each thing with a weighing scale.

③ Record your results in a table.

objects	estimate	actual mass
Example: 2 filled water bottles	1 kg	1 kg 230 g
	2 kg	
	more than 2 kg	

What is the mass of each thing?

(a)

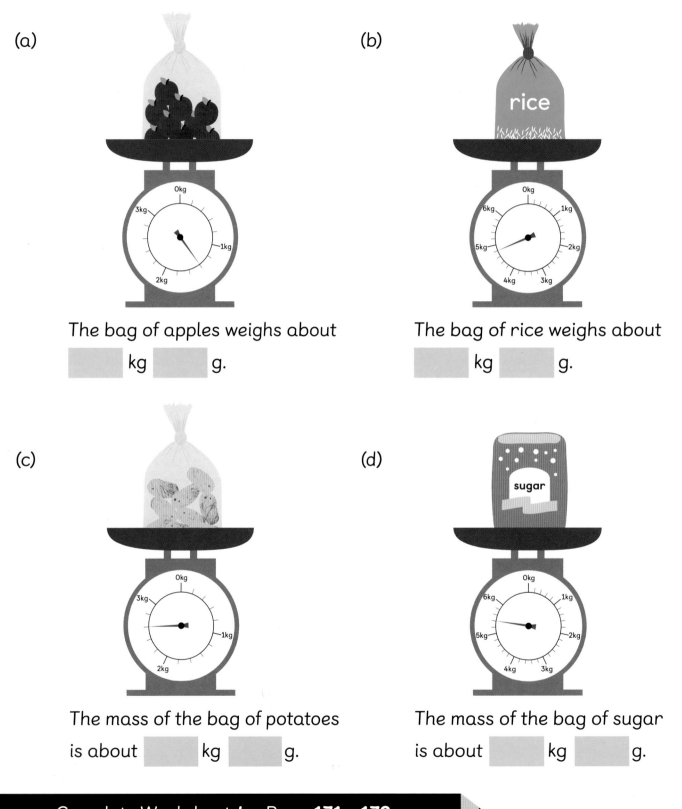

The bag of apples weighs about

[ ] kg [ ] g.

(b)

rice

The bag of rice weighs about

[ ] kg [ ] g.

(c)

The mass of the bag of potatoes

is about [ ] kg [ ] g.

(d)

sugar

The mass of the bag of sugar

is about [ ] kg [ ] g.

Complete Worksheet 4 – Page 171 – 172

Solving Word Problems

In Focus

The mass of the empty jar is about 475 g.
What is the mass of the jelly beans?

Let's Learn

The mass of the jar of jelly beans is about 900 g.

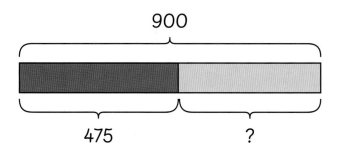

900
475   ?

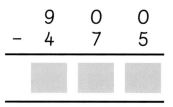

900 − 475 = 425

The mass of the jelly beans is about 425 g.

1 Emma bought 985 g of art paper.
She used 795 g of the art paper.
Find the mass of the remaining art paper.

2 A piece of luggage with clothes weighs 12 kg.
The empty luggage weighs 5 kg.
Find the mass of the clothes.

3

2 kg 275 g   1 kg 390 g

Find the total mass.

Complete Worksheet **5** – Page **173**

Solving Word Problems

In Focus

Elliott

Sam

I am twice as heavy as Elliott.

27 kg

What is the weight of Sam?

Let's Learn

Elliott — 27 kg

27

Elliott

Sam

?

$20 \times 2 = 40$

$7 \times 2 = 14$

$27 \times 2 = \boxed{}$

$$\begin{array}{r} 2\ 7 \\ \times\ \ \ 2 \\ \hline 1\ 4 \\ +\ 4\ 0 \\ \hline \end{array}$$

$27 + 27 = \boxed{}$

$27 \times 2 = 54$

Sam weighs 54 kg.

Work in groups of 4 to 6.

What you need:

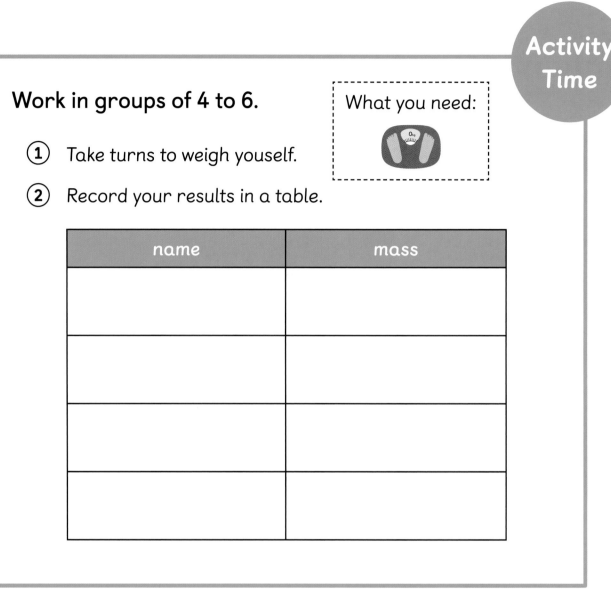

① Take turns to weigh youself.

② Record your results in a table.

name	mass

Guided Practice

1 Hannah used 56 g of chocolate to make a batch of brownies.
Ruby used twice as much chocolate to make her brownies.
How much chocolate did Ruby use?

2

40kg

 is 4 times as heavy as  .

How heavy is  ?

3 A small pack of peanuts weighs 12 g.
A large pack of peanuts weighs 3 times as much as
a small pack of peanuts.
Find the total mass of 2 small packs and
a large pack of peanuts.

Complete Worksheet **6** – Page **174 – 175**

Solving Word Problems

In Focus

Lulu had some cocoa powder.
After baking 2 cakes, she had 24 g of cocoa powder left.
She used the same amount of cocoa powder for each cake.
What is the mass of cocoa powder used for each cake?

Let's Learn

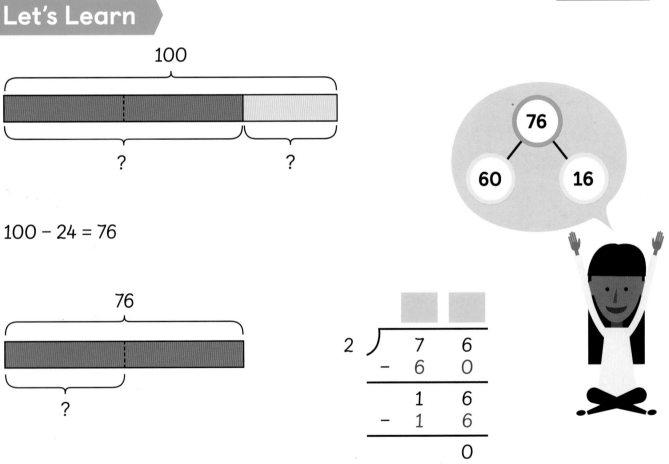

$100 - 24 = 76$

$76 \div 2 = 38$

She used 38 g of cocoa powder for each cake.

1 The five 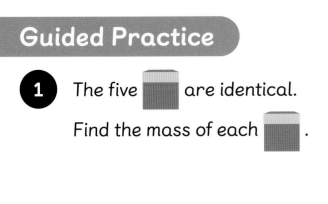 are identical.

Find the mass of each .

25g 25g 25g

2 The mass of a container with 20 identical metal balls is 480 g.
When 8 balls are removed, the mass of the container and the
remaining balls is 408 g.
What is the mass of each ball?

Complete Worksheet 7 – Page 176 – 177

Mind Workout

What does each small marking stand for?
How heavy is the bag of tomatoes?

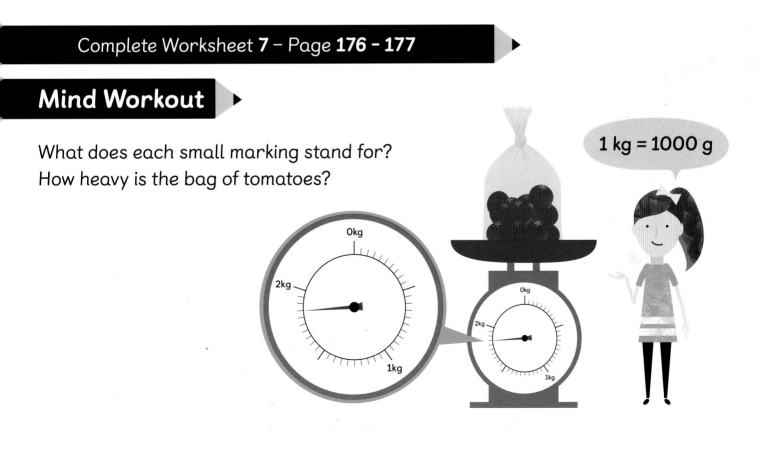

1 kg = 1000 g

Look for things that are in packets of 100 g or less.
Hold them in your hands.
You can find them at home or in the stores.

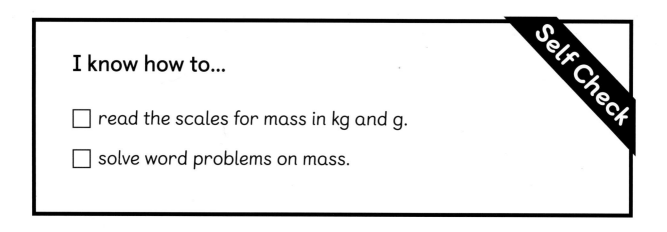

List four items that have a mass of 100 g or less.
How do you know that these items weigh 100 g or less?
Share your list with your classmates.

I know how to...

☐ read the scales for mass in kg and g.

☐ solve word problems on mass.

Self Check

Which containers have less than 1 litre of liquid?

Chapter 7
Volume

Measuring Volume in Millilitres

In Focus

The volume of liquid in the jug is 1 litre.

The remaining three containers each contain less than 1 litre of liquid.

How can we find how much liquid there is in the remaining three containers?

Let's Learn

 1 We measure volume with measuring beakers.

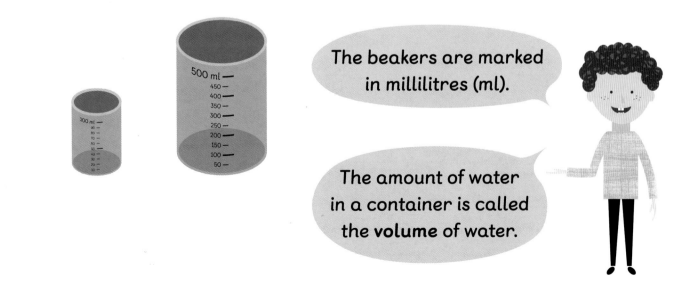

The beakers are marked in millilitres (ml).

The amount of water in a container is called the **volume** of water.

2

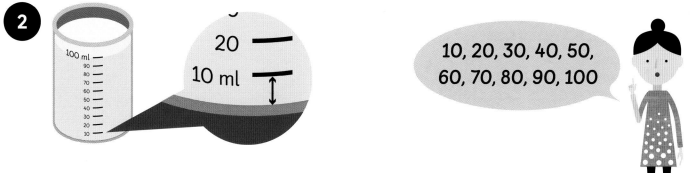

This beaker measures up to 100 millilitres.
Each marking stands for 10 millilitres.

10, 20, 30, 40, 50, 60, 70, 80, 90, 100

3

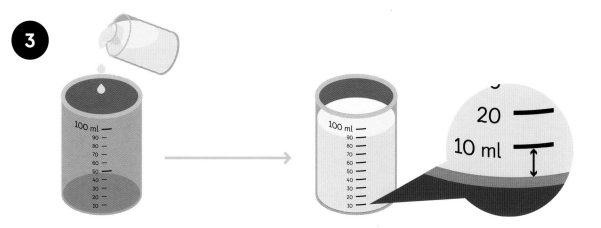

The volume of liquid in the beaker is about 90 millilitres.

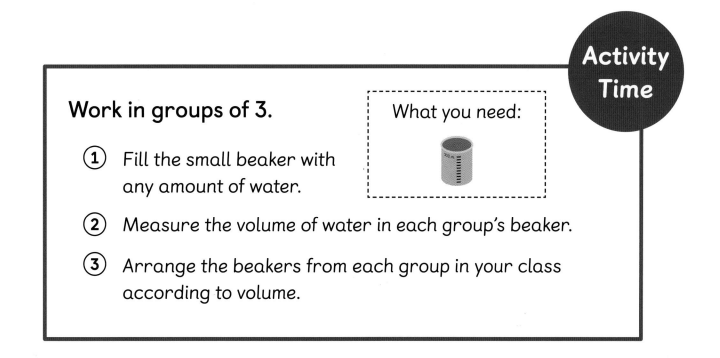

Activity Time

Work in groups of 3.

What you need:

① Fill the small beaker with any amount of water.

② Measure the volume of water in each group's beaker.

③ Arrange the beakers from each group in your class according to volume.

Guided Practice

The beakers contain coloured water.
What is the volume of water in each beaker?

(a)

The volume of coloured water in the beaker is about [ ] millilitres.

(b)

The volume of coloured water in the beaker is about [ ] millilitres.

(c)

The volume of coloured water in the beaker is about [ ] millilitres.

Complete Worksheet 1 – Page 183 ▶

Measuring Capacity in Millilitres

In Focus

How can we use this beaker to find out the amount of water the bottle can hold?

Let's Learn

1

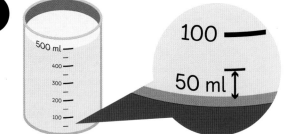

This beaker measures up to 500 millilitres.
Each marking stands for 50 millilitres.

50, 100, 150, 200, 250, 300, 350, 400, 450, 500

2

The **capacity of the bottle** is how much liquid it can hold.

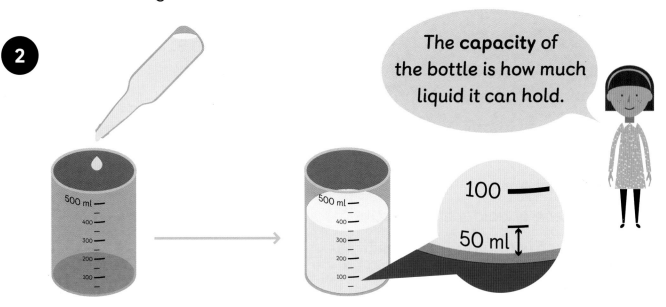

The capacity of the bottle is about 350 millilitres.

Activity Time

Work in groups of 3.

What you need:

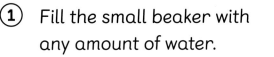

① Fill the small beaker with any amount of water.

② Measure the volume of water in each group's beaker.

③ Arrange the beakers from each group in your class according to volume.

Guided Practice

The beakers contain coloured water.
What is the volume of water in each beaker?

(a)

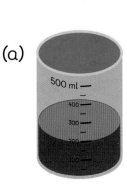

(a) The volume of coloured water in the beaker is about ▢ millilitres.

(b)

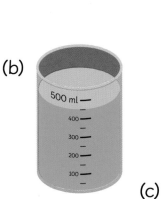

(b) The volume of coloured water in the beaker is about ▢ millilitres.

(c) The volume of coloured water in the beaker is about ▢ millilitres.

(c)

Complete Worksheet 2 – Page 184

Measuring Volume in Millilitres and Litres

In Focus

The jug holds 1 litre of liquid.
Can you show other containers that hold about 1 litre of liquid?

Let's Learn

1

The beaker is marked in litres (l).

The amount of liquid a container can hold is its **capacity**.

2

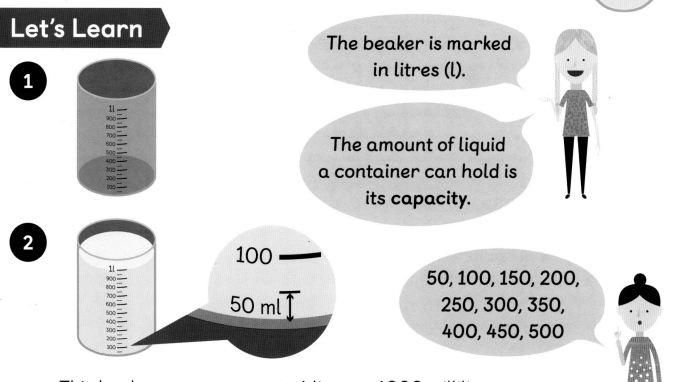

50, 100, 150, 200, 250, 300, 350, 400, 450, 500

This beaker measures up to 1 litre or 1000 millilitres.
Each marking stands for 50 millilitres.

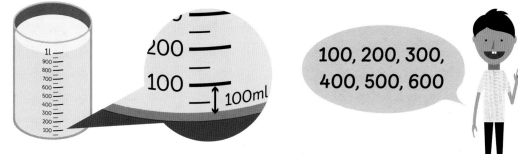

100, 200, 300, 400, 500, 600

We can also read in steps of 100 millilitres.

3 The volume of liquid in the jug is 1 **l**.
We write **ml** for millilitres.
We write **l** for litres.

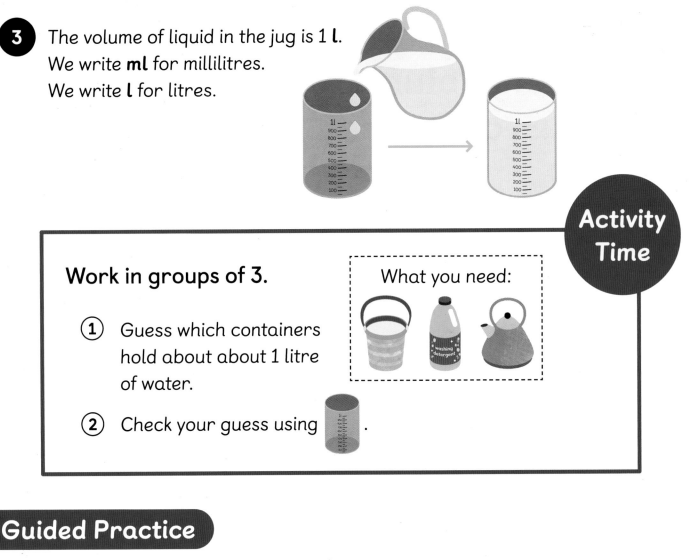

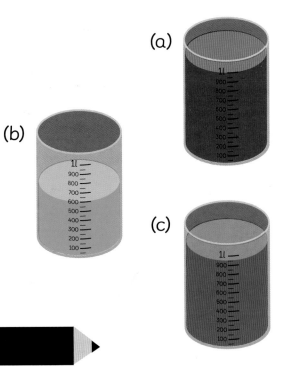

Activity Time

Work in groups of 3.

What you need:

① Guess which containers hold about about 1 litre of water.

② Check your guess using ⬛.

Guided Practice

The beakers contain coloured water.
What is the volume of water in each beaker?

(a) The volume of coloured water in the beaker is about ⬜ l.

(b) The volume of coloured water in the beaker is about ⬜ ml.

(c) The volume of coloured water in the beaker is about ⬜ ml.

Complete Worksheet **3** – Page **185**

Measuring Capacity in Millilitres and Litres

In Focus

How can we use an empty bottle and a 100 ml beaker to measure the capacity of each of the following containers?

Let's Learn

Step 1   Measure 100 ml of coloured water with the 100 ml beaker.

Step 2   Pour it into the bottle.

Step 3   Mark the water level in the bottle.

Step 4   Repeat step 1 to step 3 until the 1 l mark is reached.

Count on to make 1 l.
100 ml, 200 ml, 300 ml, 400 ml, 500 ml, 600 ml, 700 ml, 800 ml, 900 ml, 1000 ml.
1 l = 1000 ml

Step 5   Use the bottle with the markings to measure the capacity of each of the following containers.

(a)   a plastic bottle

(b)   a shampoo bottle

(c)   a plastic cup

Guided Practice

1 What is the volume of water in each beaker?

(a)

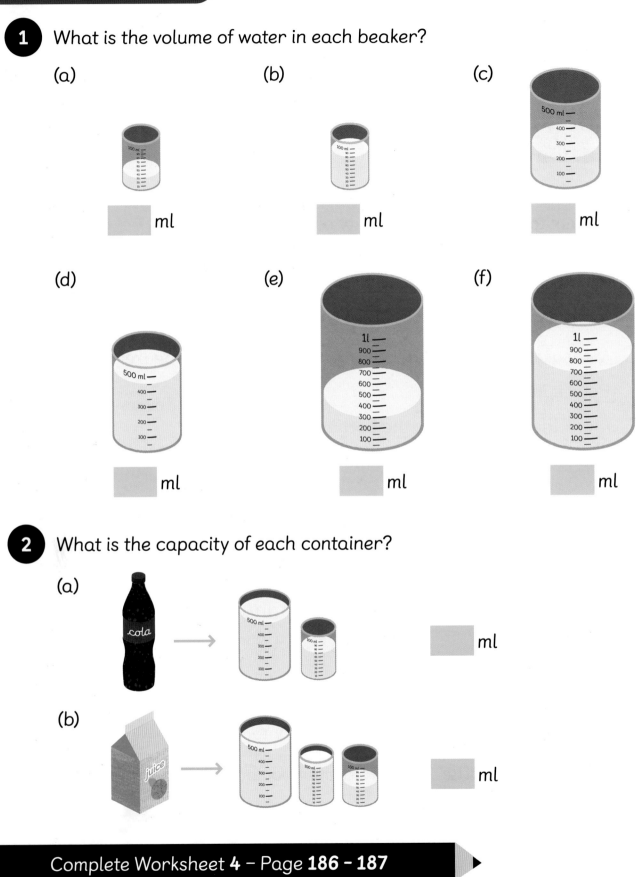

☐ ml

(b)

☐ ml

(c)

☐ ml

(d)

☐ ml

(e)

☐ ml

(f)

☐ ml

2 What is the capacity of each container?

(a)

☐ ml

(b)

☐ ml

Complete Worksheet 4 – Page **186 – 187**

Writing Volume in Litres and Millilitres

In Focus

How many millilitres make 1 litre?

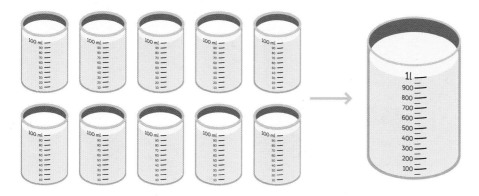

100 ml + 100 ml + 100 ml + 100 ml + 100 ml
+ 100 ml + 100 ml + 100 ml + 100 ml + 100 ml = 1000 ml

1000 millilitres make up 1 litre.
Are there other ways to make 1000 ml or 1 l?

1 l = 1000 ml

Let's Learn

1

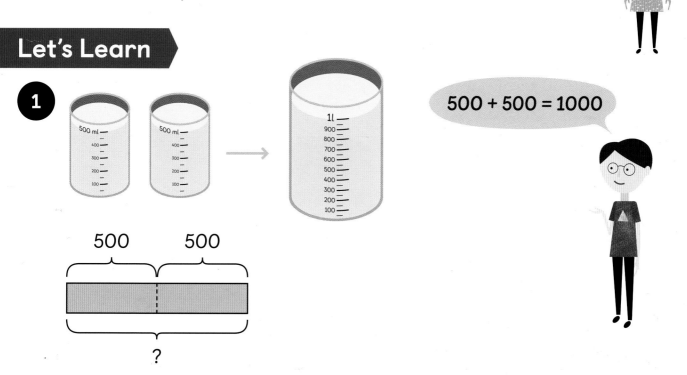

500 + 500 = 1000

2 How much more water is needed to make 1 l?

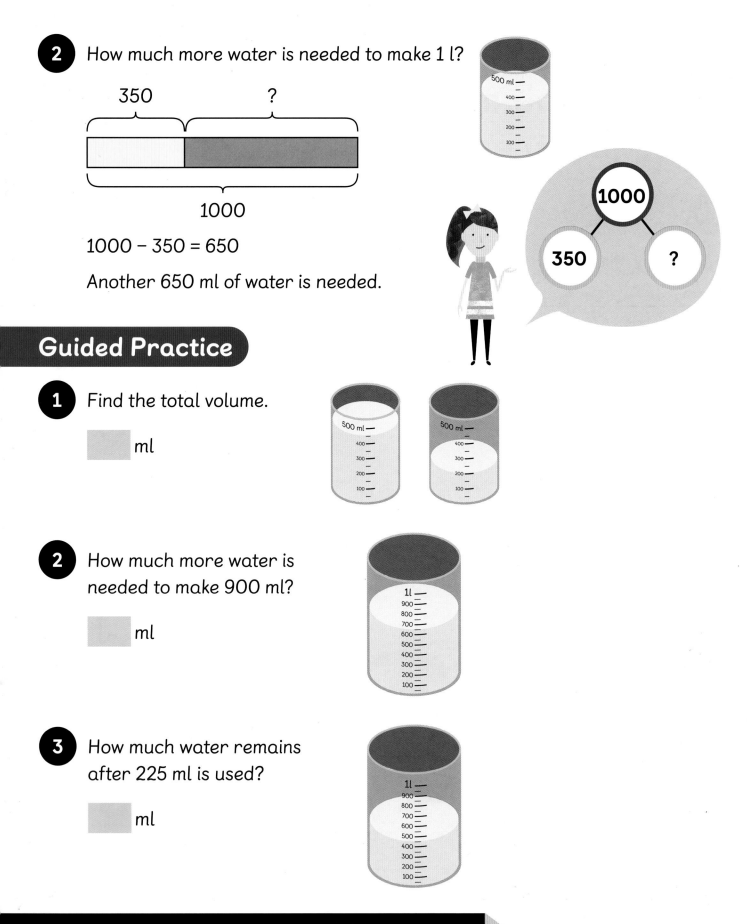

| 350 | ? |

1000

1000 − 350 = 650

Another 650 ml of water is needed.

1000

350   ?

Guided Practice

1 Find the total volume.

⬜ ml

2 How much more water is needed to make 900 ml?

⬜ ml

3 How much water remains after 225 ml is used?

⬜ ml

Complete Worksheet **5** – Page **188 – 189**

Writing Capacity in Litres and Millilitres

In Focus

Is there more than 1 litre of water in the container?

Let's Learn

This is 1 litre of water.

This is another 300 ml of water.

The container holds 1 l 300 ml of water.
It is more than 1 litre.

Activity Time

Work in groups of 4 to 5.

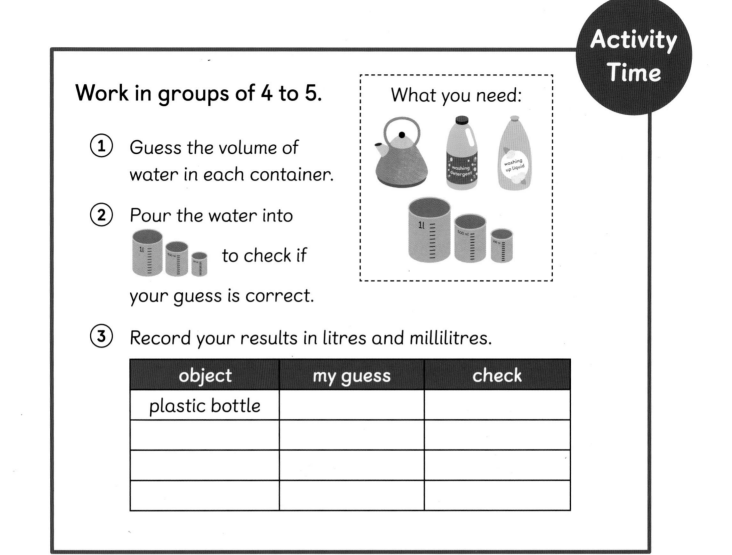

What you need:

1. Guess the volume of water in each container.

2. Pour the water into to check if your guess is correct.

3. Record your results in litres and millilitres.

object	my guess	check
plastic bottle		

Guided Practice

1

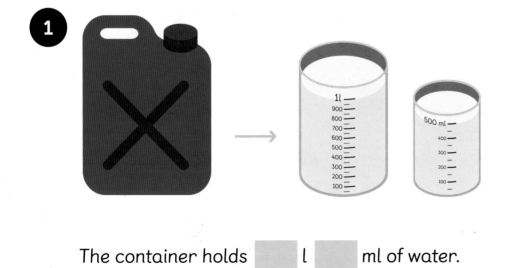

The container holds [ ] l [ ] ml of water.

2 How much water is there in the fish bowl?

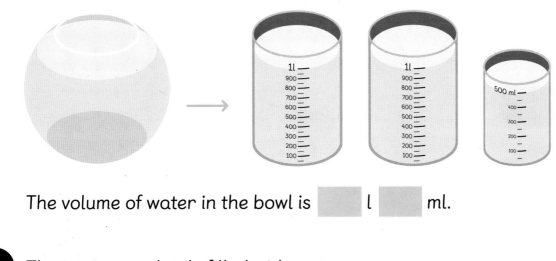

The volume of water in the bowl is [ ] l [ ] ml.

3 The jug is completely filled with water.

The capacity of the jug is [ ] l [ ] ml.

4 How much water is there in the bucket?

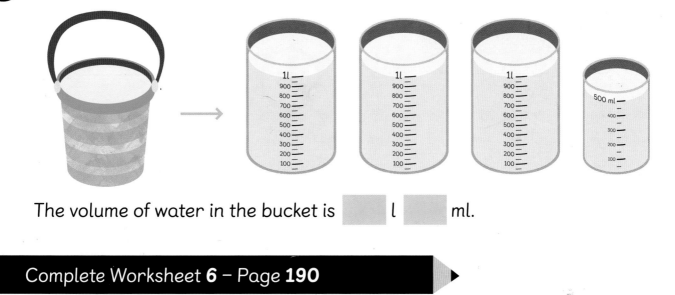

The volume of water in the bucket is [ ] l [ ] ml.

Complete Worksheet **6** – Page **190**

Solving Word Problems

In Focus

The beaker holds 125 ml less water than the bucket.
How can we find out the volume of water in the bucket?

Let's Learn

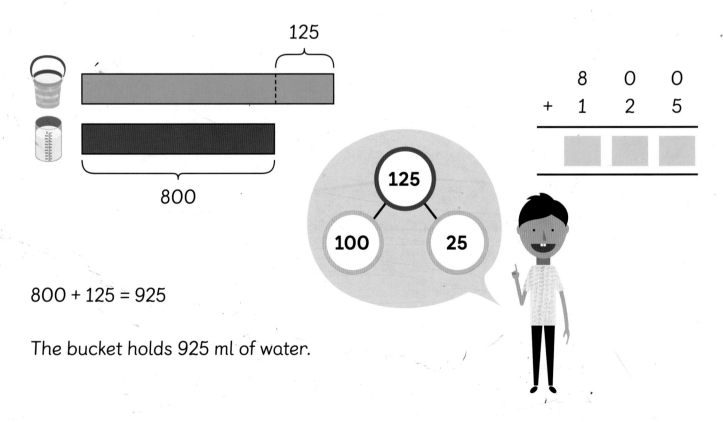

125

800

125

100   25

```
    8  0  0
 +  1  2  5
 ─────────
```

800 + 125 = 925

The bucket holds 925 ml of water.

Solve.

(a) A can holds 135 ml less water than the bottle.
Find the volume of water in the can.

(b) The bottle holds 225 ml less water than a bucket.
Find the volume of water in the bucket.

Complete Worksheet **7** – Page **191 – 192**

Solving Word Problems

In Focus

A car used 123 l of petrol last week.

The car needs 45 l more petrol this week than last week.

How can you find out how much petrol the car needs this week?

Let's Learn

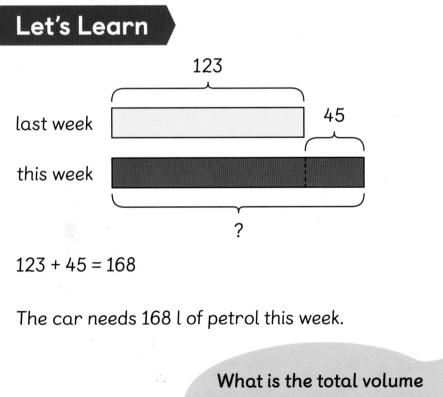

123

last week   45

this week

?

123 + 45 = 168

$$\begin{array}{r} 1\ 2\ 3 \\ +\quad 4\ 5 \\ \hline \square\ \square\ \square \end{array}$$

The car needs 168 l of petrol this week.

What is the total volume of petrol the car will use in the two weeks?

Solve.

1 A large aquarium holds 328 l of water.
A smaller aquarium holds 89 l less water than the large aquarium.
Find the volume of water in both aquariums.

2 To make a drink, Ruby used 340 ml of cold water
and some orange squash.
She used 250 ml more water than orange squash.
Find the volume of the drink she made.

Complete Worksheet **8** – Page **193 – 194**

Solving Word Problems

In Focus

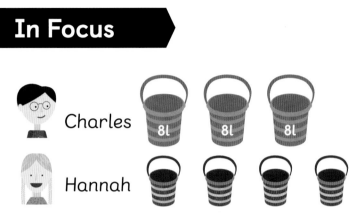

Charles' buckets hold 8 l of water each.

Charles carries twice as much water as Hannah.

How can we find out how much water Hannah carries?

Let's Learn

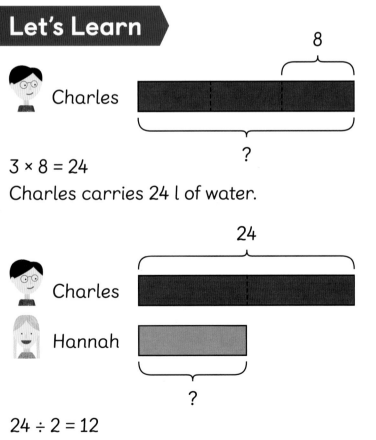

$3 \times 8 = 24$

Charles carries 24 l of water.

$24 \div 2 = 12$

Hannah carries 12 l of water.

Solve.

1 The capacity of a large bottle is twice that of a small bottle.
The capacity of the small bottle is 485 ml.
Find the capacity of the large bottle.

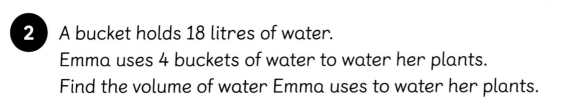

2 A bucket holds 18 litres of water.
Emma uses 4 buckets of water to water her plants.
Find the volume of water Emma uses to water her plants.

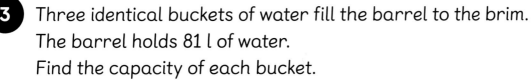

3 Three identical buckets of water fill the barrel to the brim.
The barrel holds 81 l of water.
Find the capacity of each bucket.

Complete Worksheet **9** – Page **195 – 196**

Solving Word Problems

In Focus

Each bottle has a
capacity of 38 ml.

Container

After filling 8 identical bottles, the volume of soap left is shown.
How can you find what the volume of soap in the container was at first?

Let's Learn

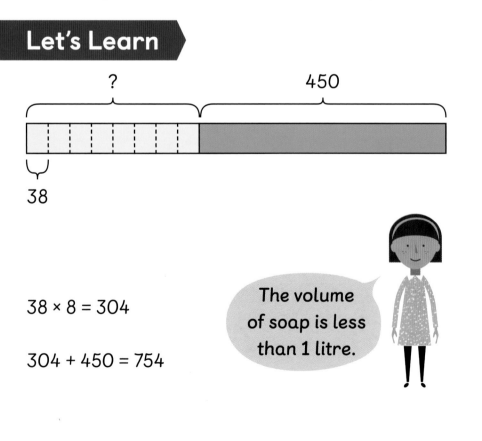

?   450

38

38 × 8 = 304

304 + 450 = 754

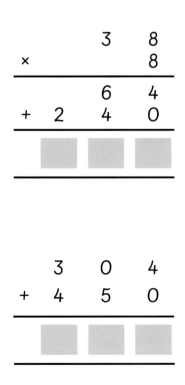

The volume
of soap is less
than 1 litre.

```
      3   8
  ×       8
      6   4
+ 2   4   0
  ▨   ▨   ▨
```

```
    3   0   4
+   4   5   0
    ▨   ▨   ▨
```

The volume of soap in the container was 754 ml.

Guided Practice

Solve.

1 There is twice as much juice in as there is in .

The total volume of juice in both containers is 6 litres.

Find the volume of juice in .

2 After filling 4 with shampoo,

there are still 722 ml of shampoo left over.
Find what the volume of shampoo was at first.

3 Ravi thinks he can fill 4 using 200 ml of shampoo.
Is he correct?

Complete Worksheet 10 – Page 197 - 198

What are the ways you can measure out
1 litre of water with these beakers?

Example

$$500 \text{ ml} + 500 \text{ ml} = 1000 \text{ ml}$$
$$= 1 \text{ l}$$

Maths Journal

We need about 2 l of water each day to stay healthy.
How much liquid do you drink every day?
Each time you take a drink, estimate and record the volume.

Do you drink enough water each day?
Share your results with your classmates.

drink	volume (ml)
water	about ___ ml
juice	about ___ ml
total	

Self Check

I know how to...

☐ measure volume in millilitres (ml) and litres (l).

☐ measure capacity in millilitres (ml) and litres (l).

☐ write volume in millilitres (ml) and litres (l).

☐ write capacity in millilitres (ml) and litres (l).

☐ solve word problems on volume and capacity.